Dancing with the Benefactors

Exploring the Wisdom of the Flower Ornament Sutra

**Other books by
Renshin Barbara Verkuilen and Taizen Dale Verkuilen
www.Firethroatpress.com**

The Tale of Zen Master Bho Li

*Dokusan with Dōgen:
Timeless Lessons in Negotiating the Way*

*Tending the Fire:
An Introspective Guide to Zen Awakening*

*Unfolding the Eightfold Path:
A Contemporary Zen Perspective*

Becoming Literate in the Process of Awakening

Dancing with the Benefactors

Exploring the Wisdom of the
Flower Ornament Sutra

Renshin Barbara Verkuilen

Firethroat Press
Madison Wisconsin

Published by
Firethroat Press, LLC
Madison, Wisconsin

www.firethroatpress.com

ISBN: 9798991279178

Cover design by Elaine Meszaros
Book design by Kira Henschel
Photography and editing by Janice Seisui Ward

Printed in the United States of America

What the Buddha Said

Once in a dream
That wasn't a dream
An Emerald Buddha appeared.
He was asked,

When the Bodhisattva of Great Compassion
Sees all the suffering of the world
How does She ever stop crying?

The Emerald Buddha replied,
You must make yourself large enough to hold it.

Renshin Barbara Verkuilen
March 5, 1945 to March 18, 2024

Table of Contents

Introduction

A number of years ago, I began the study of the Flower Ornament Sutra [*Avatamsaka* in Sanskrit, *Hua-yan* in Chinese, *Kegon* in Japanese]. The sutra is made up of 39 books. I focused on Book 39 — *Entry into the Realm of Reality* – wherein the spiritual seeker Sudhana begins his pilgrimage at Buddha's Assembly, receiving instructions from the Bodhisattva Manjushri who sends him out on his journey. Sudhana encounters 53 spiritual benefactors, each one providing pertinent and unique answers to his unresolved questions regarding the nature of an enlightening being's place in the world. Sudhana finally returns to Buddha's Assembly welcomed back after many years of seeking and finding.

I produced a number of study materials on Book 39 for personal use, summarizing the teaching of each benefactor. My wife Renshin took up the study as well, but from a completely different point of view. She had become adept in a skillful means that gave her a way to engage in an intuitive inquiry/ response method that transformed psychological and spiritual barriers. Its creator, the innovative psycho-linguistic psycho-therapist David Grove, called the process Emergent Knowledge. The original intent of Grove's Emergent Knowledge was to resolve emotional and perceptual obstructions that his psycho-therapy patients were experiencing. During their twenty-year association, and continuing after his death, Renshin modified Grove's work creating a form of Emergent Knowledge that included the original intent, then expanding it to include the process of spiritual awakening. The application of her version to the Flower Ornament Sutra benefactors produced an intuitive verbal understanding of the benefactors' teachings, and subsequently, visual collages picturing that understanding. The content of this book offers 34 examples of the benefactors' teachings in intuitive verbal and visual collage forms.

In order to grasp Renshin's largely subjective statements and images, it is necessary to investigate and gain a foundational understanding of four underlying elements:

1、 What is the Flower Ornament Sutra?

2、 What is the essence of David Grove's teachings and how did Emergent Knowledge evolve?

3、 What is Emergent Knowledge and what are the benefits of its use?

4、 What is the form of Renshin's presentation of Sudhana's engagement with each benefactor?

WHAT IS THE FLOWER ORNAMENT SUTRA?[1]
The Flower Ornament Sutra contains 39 books of vast, rich, and grandiose Buddhist teaching, held in high esteem by all Buddhist schools concerned with universal liberation. It is a work of stunning imagination capable of transforming one's perspective from concept to the immediacy of metaphorical understanding. The function of the sutra is to affirm the infinity of the path, and inspire practitioners to take up the mission of cultivating wisdom and compassion.

It is not known when and by whom the Flower Ornament Sutra was compiled. Scholars believe that the first written copies appeared in Northern India during the 1st and 2nd century CE, arising from the oral tradition that asserted the sutra contained the sermons Shakyamuni Buddha preached during the first three weeks after his enlightenment. The sutra was transmitted to China and Japan during the 1st millennium, where it formed the basis of the Hua-yan and Kegon philosophical schools. D. T. Suzuki described the sutra's relationship with the Zen schools in his assertion, "Zen is the practical consummation of Buddhist thought in China, and the Kegon is its theoretical culmination…the philosophy of Zen is Kegon and the teaching of Kegon bears fruit in the life of Zen."

Book 39 is the story of Sudhana and his encounter with 53 benefactors. Sudhana approached Buddha's Assembly, and was given the opportunity to ask for guidance. He said to Manjushri, "Noble One, please give me a full explanation of how an enlightening being is to study the practice of enlightening beings, how an enlightening being is to accomplish it?"

Then Manjushri said to Sudhana, "It is good that you think, having set your heart on supreme enlightenment, that you should find out the practice of enlightening beings. One should respectfully follow the appropriate instructions of spiritual benefactors, without interruption. South of here is a country called Ramavaranta; there is a mountain there called Sugriva, where a monk named Meghashri lives. Go to him and ask how an enlightening being should learn the conduct of enlightening beings and how to apply it; how to fulfill, purify, carry out, follow, keep to, and expand the practice of enlightening beings, and how an enlightening being is to fulfill the sphere of universally good action. That spiritual friend will tell you about the sphere of universally good conduct."

The balance of the text of the sutra documents Sudhana's encounters with 50 spiritual benefactors and the three guiding principles of Maitreya, Manjushri, and Samantabhadra with whom he visits one after the other.

The 50 benefactors are presented in five groups of ten: The Ten Abodes, The Ten Practices, The Ten Dedications, The Ten Stages, and The Ten Steps of the Eleventh Stage. *Entry into the Realm of Reality* describes in detail the teachings of the Five Ranks, with each group of ten expounding on an individual rank, with The Ten Abodes chronicling the first rank and so on. Each benefactor provides a basic teaching, offering new ways to achieve meditative awareness. A diligent and committed study of the material offers a remarkable opportunity for practitioners to follow Sudhana on his spiritual journey and, like him, awaken this vast array of teachings within themselves.[2]

The sutra's text is written from the perspective of the interpenetration of the Personal (*shi*) and Universal (*li*) Aspects of Mind. In reading the text, we must deliver ourselves into the intuitive world and attempt to understand and engage with the dream-like information, much like we would seek to grasp the meaning of a metaphor. But this metaphor is not a comparison.

The usual understanding of a metaphor is that it is a poetic tool by which meaning is conveyed through comparison of one thing to another. The sutra text describes the mutually beneficial interaction of the personal and universal aspects of reality. Here, the metaphor contains both the symbol and what is symbolized, an intuitive realization of the truth of the unity of the Personal and Universal Aspects of Mind. In order to grasp the meaning of unity, it is necessary to transcend the notion that metaphors in Buddhism convey only a kind of likeness standing apart from "reality as it is." Zen Master Dōgen wrote, "*Being like* does not express resemblance, *being like* is concrete existence." Metaphoric images and verbal articulations are concrete existence itself. (See "Metaphors in the Buddhist Process of Awakening" in the Background Material)

Hence, the sutra text invites the reader/practitioner into the world of concrete existence, not a "nothing but," "just your imagination," or impenetrable gibberish. This view is consistent with how "*it is like*" is used in Zen Master Tung-Shan's *The Song of the Jewel Mirror Awareness*. "*It is like*" is not pointing out an idea or concept. Rather, "*it is like*" is the faculty of intuition, Buddhist wisdom itself. When Master Tung-Shan uses the phrase "*it is like*", he is expressing the direct realization of the intimacy of the Personal and Universal Aspects of Mind. Intimacy here is used in the way Taizan Maezumi Roshi meant when he taught, "… intimacy is simply realizing that your true nature and the phenomenal world are meeting right here, now, as your life." Maezumi Roshi's statement points out that the study of the Flower Ornament Sutra is not philosophical but experiential in nature, offering familiarity with the benefactors' efforts and teachings so that they come alive in our understanding, being, and behavior.

WHAT IS THE ESSENCE OF DAVID GROVE'S TEACHINGS AND HOW DID EMERGENT KNOWLEDGE EVOLVE?[3]

David Grove was born in New Zealand in December 1950 of bi-cultural Māori/British parents. As a counseling psychotherapist, his association with Neuro-linguistic Programming influenced his early work, where he became interested in traumatic memories and phobias. While observing very carefully what was happening, he noticed, "If I didn't force people when they were talking, they would naturally start using metaphors to describe their experience." From that understanding he devised Clean Language and Metaphor Therapy, methods of inquiry that did not interfere with the naturally arising metaphoric information. The method of inquiry he developed kept the healing process information-centered rather than being shaped by a therapist or client-imposed analysis or interpretation.

Renshin attended a seminar on Grove's Metaphor Therapy, later writing about her experience:

> *"In 1989, I attended a seminar on Metaphor Therapy presented by David Grove in Milwaukee, Wisconsin. The seminar demonstrated how the root causes of trauma, depression, and anxiety could be resolved. Having practiced Zen meditation (Zazen) for almost twenty years at that time, I recognized similarities between the methods of Zen and Metaphor Therapy. Both are based on an all-inclusive nonduality, the focal point of which is a non-intrusive inquiry into the nature of self. Later, after reviewing my notes, I became even more convinced of my initial insight."*

Grove's facilitator-based techniques required a high level of expertise on the part of the facilitator and substantial preparation time for the client/practitioner. Later, Grove developed Emergent Knowledge that could be successfully accomplished without a facilitator, while staying true to his basic premises. This process offers a skillful means that practitioners can easily learn and creatively employ, with intuitive understanding at its heart.

Elements of these methods were taken up and over a 34-year period, adapted and tested by Renshin and her community members. She combined Emergent Knowledge with Zen practice yielding a process that contains the means to access and develop the transformative power of Buddhist awakening. Some of the means contained within Emergent Knowledge are:

- Ability to identify and address the fundamental misperception of the makeup of the self
- An introspective method called the Resolution Sequence that comprehensively describes the three-fold process of awakening
- A universal symbolic system that illustrates the process of awakening
- Incorporation of Emergent Knowledge into study of Buddhist texts that facilitates speed and integration of learning

Emergent Knowledge and Zen Practice requires a prerequisite Buddhist education to understand and apply. Later Renshin developed Enhanced Emergent Knowledge, which removed all technical and psychological terminology while retaining its essence, making many of its transformational abilities open to all.

WHAT IS EMERGENT KNOWLEDGE AND WHAT ARE THE BENEFITS OF ITS USE?[3]

Renshin asserted that Emergent Knowledge accesses the same level of insight as Mitsugo, a Buddhist practice Gudo Nishijima describes in his introduction to Fascicle 51, in Zen Master Dōgen's Shobogenzo:

> *"Mitsugo means secret talk, that is, something communicated directly without sound. In Buddhism it is said that there is secret talk that can be recognized and understood even though it has no sound. So "secret talk" suggests the existence of intuitive perception. It is a fact that we can sometimes discover meaning, or*

secrets, without receiving any external stimuli, but we need not see the fact as particularly mystical.[4]

Emergent Knowledge's inquiry/response facilitates the conscious awareness of the intuitive inner dialogue, the innate rapport between the Personal and Universal Aspects of Mind. Emergent Knowledge's intuitive principle is consistent with the teachings of the Flower Ornament Sutra and the Yogacara School of Buddhism.

The Yogacara School greatly influenced the development of Zen Buddhism. Yogacara taught the three aspects of the process of awakening: 1) resolving vexations caused by conditioned states, 2) refining and integrating the freedom from conditioned states, and 3) living that freedom. These three are integral to Zen practice.

Grove's Emergent Knowledge approach focused in the first aspect of removing vexations, their resolution granting freedom from their tyranny. Renshin added the two other Yogacara aspects when adapting Emergent Knowledge, fashioning its form, content, and method in accord with Zen practice. The second aspect incorporates the dedication of the Buddhist practitioner to integrate the newly found freedom. With release from the negative influences of the vexations, the Universal and Personal Aspects of Mind beneficially interact, refining the attributes of the Personal. The third aspect realizes authentic personhood by living that freedom. When the three aspects of the process of awakening are accurately and correctly utilized, vexations are cleansed, and the original purity of mind manifests as transformed harmonious activity.

WHAT IS THE FORM OF RENSHIN'S PRESENTATION OF SUDHANA'S ENGAGEMENT WITH EACH BENEFACTOR?

Renshin's way of studying the Flower Ornament Sutra is centered within intuitive dialogue. She applied Enhanced Emergent Knowledge which produced a verbal depiction of the intuitive engagement with that benefactor's teaching. Then, she took that information and the teachings of Visual Journaling to create collages that portrayed her visual intuition.[5]

Each benefactor's presentation consists of the following:

Emergent Knowledge – verbal intuition

- The listing of number and name of the benefactor
- The benefactor's living location in the world and their basic teaching
- In Italics: The author's Want Statement or an excerpt from the text that conveys the heart of the Want Statement
- Six Emergent Knowledge inquiries and responses
- The WDIKN Proclamation Statement

Visual Journaling – pictorial intuition
- The complex intuitive imagery that arose from the Proclamation Statement

The italics portion of each of Renshin's presentations describes the "want" that she desired to understand, to make her own, to resolve an emotional or cognitive obstruction, or to know how to embody and share a teaching with others. She created a Want Statement (a statement of intention), then used it as the basis for her inquiries as listed below:

1、 What is the first thing I know about that? Record response.

2、 And what else? Record response.

3、 And what else? Record response.

4、 And what else? Record response.

5、 And what else? Record response.

6、 And what else? Record response.

7、 And **what do I know now** that I didn't know before?
Record response.

The answer to the WDIKN question is known as the Proclamation Statement.

Emergent Knowledge inquiry asks six questions based on the identified Want Statement. This method remains pure and unadulterated if practitioners maintain the unity of the inquiry-response process by avoiding analyzing the intuitive non-conceptual information as it arises.

These inquiries are the source of verbal intuition. Each inquiry/response is an awakening. The six inquiry/responses are summarized in the Proclamation Statement by asking and answering, "What do I know now that I didn't know before?" With further reflection on the Proclamation Statement and a measure of artistic endeavor, the intuitive information becomes visually represented in the collage.

Renshin was able to converse with images in a similar intuitional manner as Emergent Knowledge. The Proclamation Statement served as the root in forming of the images. The images were not guess-work or happenstance, but a product of awareness of the fundamental nature of the Proclamation Statement. If you closely inquire into the meaning of the Proclamation Statement, letting it seep in, going beyond the intellectual boundary that we impose on ourselves, the image may lose its sense of arbitrariness and convey the unity of the verbal Proclamation Statement and the visual collage.

The Emergent Knowledge process engages with the fundamental principle of Buddhism: wisdom. What is wisdom? Real wisdom is the intuitive-mind, the faculty of intuition, wherein the inconceivable Universal Aspect of Mind is revealed and made realizable. Renshin's verbal responses and collages are examples of intuitive wisdom, products of "secret talk," that is, something communicated directly. To engage in the inquiry and response is to engage with your own intuition, your own wisdom. In *Dancing with the Benefactors* Renshin invites you to become familiar with and to participate intimately in the joyous teaching of the Flower Ornament Sutra.

Dancing with the Benefactors

Exploring the Wisdom of the Flower Ornament Sutra

Flower Ornament Sutra

What is an Enlightening Being?

*I want to understand the Flower Ornament Sutra term
"enlightening being?"*

1、 Because of the gerund ending, it is always a present
   moment activity

2、 This means they are perpetually engaged in
   working for the benefit of others, as it is always
   the present moment.

3、 Their activities may be grand or small

4、 Whenever anyone is engaged in an activity with the
   thought of "others" they are an enlightening being.

5、 Practice *seeing* others as enlightening beings.
   What did you learn from them? How did they leave
   you feeling?

6、 Practice becoming really aware of others in your
   interactions with them. Make it personal, heart to
   heart.

WDIKN:
When oneself or others are present in the moment, they have
the possibility [depending on the nature of their behavior] of
influencing the situation as an enlightening being. Once again,
awareness is the key.

(This first Emergent Knowledge inquiry/response does not have an image because
examples of what an "Enlightening Being" consists is portrayed in the following 34
collages. Renshin began her questioning with the same need as Sudhana)

.

THE TEN ABODES

Benefactor One
Meghashri "Glorious Clouds"

Male Monk – Inspiration and Initial Determination
Cessation of Opinion and Argument

"He will tell you of the immense,
intense power of the root of goodness."

1、 Goodness feeds on itself, yet…

2、 It is fragile and we must nurture it like a hen on a
nest.

3、 Follow your unselfconscious heart

4、 Allow the transformation to deepen

5、 Witness it operating everywhere

6、 Let goodness and compassion bring joy

WDIKN:
Wisely choose where you place your attention.

Benefactor Two
Sagaramegha "Ocean Cloud"

Male Monk - Altruism & Compassion
There is no place to attain Buddhahood outside the ocean of
birth and death.

"Wisdom is adorned by the principle
of the state of non-contention."

1. Non-contention is nonattachment to opinion and
   judgment even though they arise.
2. It is radical acceptance of the circumstance and
   allows for authentic response.
3. Non-contention affords energy to initiate change
   quickly.
4. It imbues one with equanimity
5. It eliminates fear
6. It is the base by which to assess the circumstance

WDIKN:
Hold both sides … act with conviction … be prepared to
change

Benefactor Three
Supratishthita "Well Established"

Male Monk - Practice
Supratishthita found the door of unobstructed liberation. The ocean of birth and death turns into the ocean of knowledge.

The Unobstructed door "Ultimate Non-obstruction"

1、 This is a step past non-contention

2、 It is how to go beyond obstruction

3、 It is the essential door to freedom

4、 It is like a revolving door one passes through with each experience

5、 It is practicing with death as your guide

6、 If you practice with it, you can die without fear

WDIKN:
Non-obstruction is living in harmony with Reality

Benefactor Four
Megha "Cloud"

Lay Male Teacher - Noble Birth
A layperson's place in the world provides teaching and example a monk cannot provide.
When it is said that phenomena exist, each one is inherently empty; when it is said that phenomena do not exist, that does not destroy appearances.

Enlightening beings do what is difficult to do; it is hard to get to actually see them; ... always seeing spiritual benefactors.

1、 Practice witnessing synchronicity

2、 The world around you manifests reality

3、 Remain open beyond what you think you know

4、 Ask. How does what you are experiencing reflect how you are?

5、 Balance pain with gratitude

6、 Develop the eye that sees "goodness"

WDIKN:
Bring the Buddha-realm to the mundane and the mundane to the Buddha-realm.

Benefactor Five
Muktaka "The Liberated One"

Male Layman – Skill in Means
Buddha is the accord of the inner mind with reality.

"I realize, I am mindful, that all enlightenment principles of enlightening beings are based on one's own mind." "Spiritual communion with the cosmos, and knowledge of subtle communion with all ages, all are based on one's own mind."

1、 One's experience is all one really has
2、 The mind is vast and multifaceted
3、 Be vigilant to the ruts where the mind strays
4、 Protect the aspiration to awaken
5、 Stretch yourself in new experiences
6、 Enjoy the playfulness and humor you are capable of

WDIKN:
Practice must include a deep appreciation of all the capacities of one's mind.

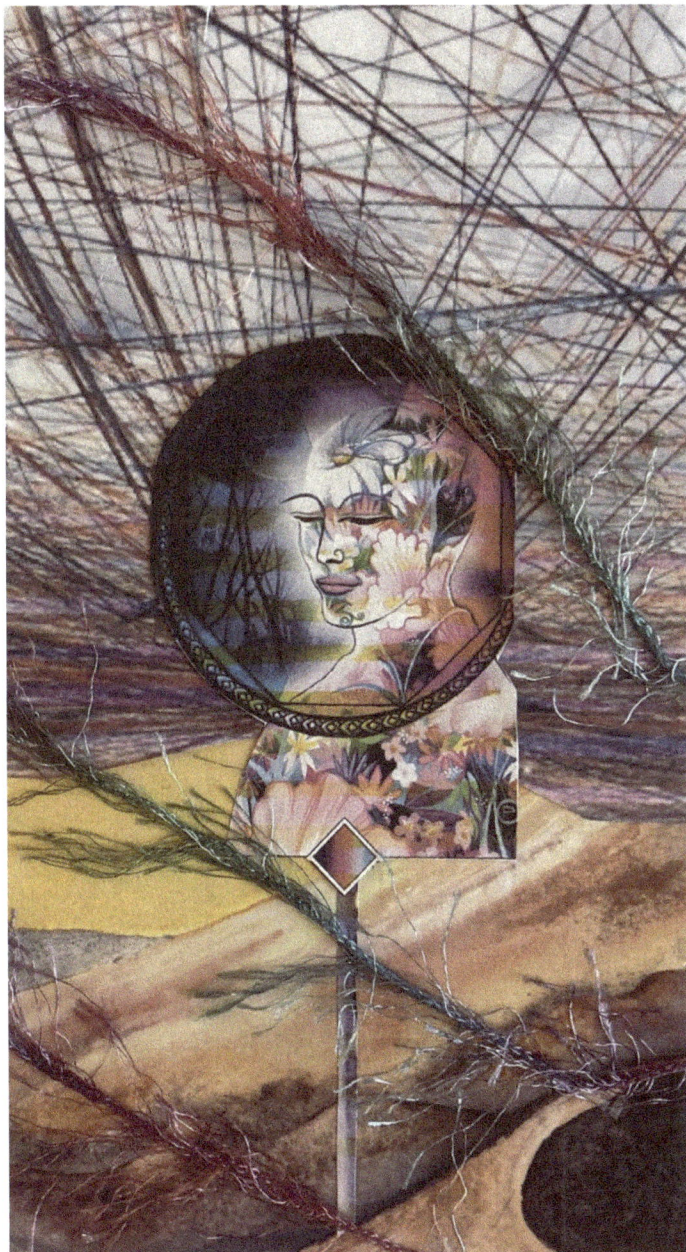

Benefactor Six
Saradhvaja "Ocean Banner"

Male Monk - Correct State of Mind

"Directing sentient beings to guard their senses."

1、 Become aware of the stimulus you receive and the place it goes in you.

2、 Question the legitimacy of that response.

3、 Find the thread and trace from beginning to end.

4、 Be careful of what you allow in – limit negative influences

5、 Discern the intent of others

6、 Fill your senses with beauty – sight, sound, smell, taste, and touch

WDIKN:
Practice #6 more consciously. The rest will follow.

WDIKN:
This is difficult work because of the "dream" of experience I see as reality.

Benefactor Seven
Asha "Ubiquitous Adornment"

Female Lay Person – Non-regression
Recognition of the original unity of the essence of life and
death comes from using the eighty-four thousand afflictions as
guides.

*I would like to understand what the "state of sorrowless well
being" means.*

1、 It is an enormous accomplishment

2、 It is dependent on selflessness

3、 It is Matsuoka's "you will learn to suffer in another
way."

4、 When gripped by sorrow, seek to discern attachment to self.

5、 Do not confuse grief for attachment to self

6、 Discern how sorrow is related but separate from
grief

WDIKN:
There is a layer of confusion I must clarify between sorrow and
grief. Grief is the key.

WDIKN:
I must learn to understand the deep nuances of grief. It must
become the source of energy not depletion of it.

Benefactor Eight
Bhishmottaranirghosha
"He Who Utters the Fearsome Sound"

Male Seer – Youthful Nature and Innocence
Effortless knowledge is an unshakable liberation.

Sudhana – his mind invulnerable and immune to the power of all demons

1、 Demons are our own negative thinking

2、 They are powerful and shape-shifters

3、 Recognize them by their emotional effects

4、 Cultivate the energy to turn away from them immediately

5、 Create or use a mantra to protect your mind

6、 Form this beneficial habit and become invulnerable and immune

WDIKN:
I can use this simple remedy to stay alert. I want to cultivate this beneficial habit.

Benefactor Nine
Jayoshmayatana "Victorious Heat"

Male Brahmin - Spiritual Prince
Used knowledge to overcome the poisonous heat of emotional
    afflictions.
Tranquility opens the gate of inconceivability.

*"Climb this razor-edge-path mountain and jump from there
into the fire—thus will your enlightening practice be purified. "*

1、 The razor's edge is the balance between the two
    truths of personal and universal knowing.

2、 The fire is emptiness

3、 Purification is staying with both truths and not
    succumbing to the truth of only one.

4、 My task is to remember the emptiness of the world-
    ly realm of appearances without losing the ability
    to respond to those appearances

5、 Cultivate the truth of universal knowing

WDIKN:
This is the task I must undertake. I don't understand why
from where I am now, but this is why I need the changes we are
initiating.

In response to the comment, "climb this razor-edge-path mountain and jump from there into the fire – thus will your enlightening practice be purified, "Sudhana thought, 'It is hard to avoid the situations that are inopportune for enlightenment; it is hard to be human; it is hard to remove error and doubt about the right opportunity; it is hard to find a buddha in the world; it is hard to have all one's faculties in order; it is hard to get to hear the truth; it is hard to meet people of truth; it is hard to find genuine spiritual benefactors; it is hard to get genuine guidance and instruction; it is hard to live right in the human world; it is hard to carry out truth in all respects. Might this not be a demon?"

Benefactor Ten
Maitrayani "Maiden Kind Conduct"

Young Girl – Courageous Invigoration
Freedom from attraction to habits and spontaneous compassion.
Supreme knowledge of Wisdom and Compassion.

Perceiving all sentient beings as void of self or inherent identity

1、 I must see interdependence of all beings and phenomenon

2、 Recognize the cause for arisings and conditions for existence

3、 Note the varying lengths of duration as impermanence

4、 Study impermanence in yourself – life history to present moment experience

5、 Self includes environment

6、 Until this is persistent awareness practice observing it periodically throughout the day or night

WDIKN:
I need to make perceiving this a practice. If done correctly the result will be becoming aware of the perpetual newness of myself, and my surroundings

THE TEN PRACTICES

Benefactor Eleven
Sudarshana "Three Eyes"

Male Mendicant - Pure conduct, practice of joy
Three eyes: eye of knowledge that observes faculties, the objective eye that knows principles, and the eye of wisdom that understands dualities.

How does one practice joy?

1、 Use your senses to seek beauty
2、 Catch and stop negative habits of thought
3、 Be more present with your body
4、 See the moment
5、 Open to the newness of each moment
6、 Stay silent in action [watch for arising negative opinions]

WDIKN:
Cultivating joy isn't difficult but it is another awareness practice.

Dancing with the Benefactors

Benefactor Twelve
Indriyeshvara "Fragrance of Morality"

Young Boy
Beneficent practice – The discipline of practice removes barriers to tranquility and happiness.

How should I understand the "treasure of will that is rare and most difficult to obtain?'

1、 Bring all your thoughts to your intention to awaken

2、 Guard against negative memories

3、 Guard against unnecessary judgment of the present

4、 Guard against thinking you know the future

5、 Act immediately on all generous inclinations

6、 Do not become discouraged by old habits of mind

WDIKN:
Staying truly present in the moment attains the six steps above without effort

Dancing with the Benefactors

Having broken open the doors of confinement
in the city of mundane existence.

1、 The doors of confinement are fear, judgment, doubt, and insecurity about what you know.

2、 Remember that each moment is fleeting and unrepeatable

3、 Stay alert

4、 Maintain equilibrium internally

5、 Be kind in response to the world

6、 Be kind in response to yourself

WDIKN:
Stay still. Maintain gentleness with your imagined failings.

Benefactor Thirteen
Prabhuta "Perfected"

Female Layperson – Ocean Foundation
Transcendent acceptance - impartially embraces the world
without judgment or preference.

How do I understand "the vessel that never runs out?"

1、 Emptiness is the vessel

2、 It is the undying energy of the universe

3、 The undying energy "never runs out" even when
   appearances pass from existence

4、 Learn to rejoice in the transitory

5、 Guard against fear from the trauma of the mundane
   world

6、 Observe the choreography of the natural world

WDIKN:
It is time to transfer my attention and find refuge in nature
which is the same as the realm of the Buddhas

Dancing with the Benefactors

Benefactor Fourteen
Vidvan "Knower"

Male Layperson – Indomitability
Contemplating the emptiness of phenomena produces liberation and quells worldly attachments.

What does it mean to be "lifted out of worldliness ... and to cross over the wildness of the mundane whirl?"

1、 Lifted out of worldliness means to recognize that what we see isn't all there is.

2、 This lessens attachment to phenomena that is ever changing.

3、 We must respond to the world understanding that what we do may change everything we think we know about our life.

4、 Connect with wholesome intentions before acting.

5、 Be prepared to act alone and don't judge others.

6、 Cultivate tenderness for the beauty of the world.

WDIKN:
The mundane whirl is seductive. One must fully participate without attachment. Cross over is nonattachment to the whirl of mundane phenomena.

Dancing with the Benefactors

Benefactor Fifteen
Ratnachuda "Jewel Topknot"

Male Teacher – Non-confusion
Confused states of mind are uprooted, and the source and power of compulsive habits are identified and eliminated.

The "door of transcendent wisdom called invincible matrix."

1、 The door of transcendent wisdom is opened when one includes everything

2、 Transcendent wisdom is beyond duality

3、 Transcendent wisdom cannot be corrupted

4、 The invincible matrix is comprised of the seen and unseen elements that make up one's life.

5、 Live what you know without forgetting what you don't know

6、 This is the path to authenticity

WDIKN:
Transcendent wisdom does not make one brave. One must be courageous to cultivate transcendent wisdom … living within the invincible matrix.

Benefactor Sixteen
Samantanetra "Universal Eye"

Male Teacher – Good Manifestation
Transcendent wisdom sends its roots deep into the depths of
being providing nourishment, stability, and direction.

*How does one develop the degree of "commitment and
determination required for enlightenment"?*

1、 One must be diligent with patience for oneself.

2、 One must be unmoved by the problems of the
world.

3、 One must see the problems of the world as
evidence of the Buddha's truth.

4、 Witnessing the evidence of the Buddha's truth, that
suffering is caused by fundamental ignorance,
strive to respond to suffering with understanding of
its cause.

5、 Counter suffering where you can with deep
kindness

6、 Deep kindness is seeing.

WDIKN:
Commitment and determination are acquired one instance at a
time. Respond from the deepest understanding you are capable
of.

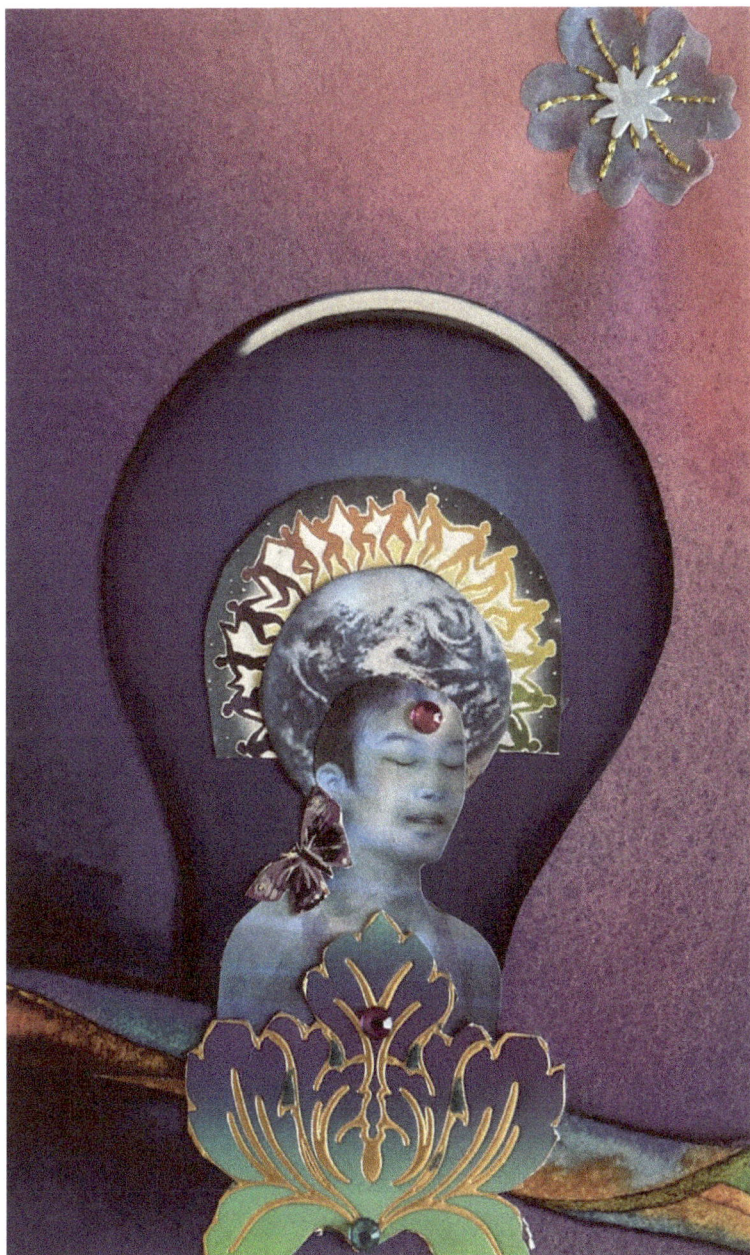

Benefactor Seventeen
Anala "Tireless"

Male King - "Tireless" means motivation without consideration of self. Wisdom that is free of personal gain enters into the world of compassion

How should I understand that *"the practices of enlightening beings are like magical creations, who know that all worlds are like reflections, who comprehend that the nature of things is like a dream?"*

1、 Accept this statement as true even though you don't understand it.

2、 Open your heart to the "magic" of the ordinary

3、 Know that when you recognize the "magic" of the ordinary, it reflects your open heart

4、 When the heart is sore it's the opposite of tireless. It is ok to rest. It is necessary.

5、 Watch for small signs of the heart opening again.

6、 Tears of grief may be the portal.

WDIKN:
One must accept the truth of one's state of being without judgment or attachment. "Turning away and touching are both wrong." There is no way "beyond" than "through."

Benefactor Eighteen
Mahaprabha "Great Light"

Male King – "Great Light" expresses the Mahayana teachings of impermanence, interdependence, and the understanding that all phenomena express universal truth.

"Furthermore, no one goes away from me intimidated, threatened or frightened. If any poor people lacking in means of subsistence come to me ...I open the royal storehouse to them and allow them to take from there ... whatever they need, things they would otherwise get involved in wrongdoing to get." Mahaprabha acts from pure benevolence.

I would like to deepen my understanding of benevolence.

1、 Benevolence is an attitude of anticipatory kindness
2、 Benevolence is giving deeply; that which others don't even know they need
3、 Seeing others with acceptance
4、 It's the tender heart of a child
5、 Open to tenderness with beauty and music
6、 Heal your own child's heart

WDIKN:
Learn kindness towards yourself. Learn from, and forgive, your mistakes.

Benefactor Nineteen
Achala "Immovable

Female Layperson - Good Teaching
Achola is called "The Immovable" because of her spiritual power to stay true and unaffected by the world.

What does it mean to stay true and be unaffected by the world?

1、 Staying true is not losing one's connection to oneself
2、 Staying true requires perpetual assessment of what one thinks they know
3、 Staying true is dealing with one's limiting and habitual conditioned states
4、 To be unaffected by the world means not needing recognition or validation from others
5、 Unaffected by the world does not mean being uninvolved with the world
6、 Staying true requires self-acceptance at the deepest level, warts and all

WDIKN:
Staying true affords one equanimity and composure for dealing with the world.

Benefactor Twenty
Sarvagamin "Going Everywhere"

Male Mendicant
"Learners are called outsiders as long as they have not yet
entered into the real universe, where there is interpenetration of
noumenon [sacred] and phenomena [mundane]."

How should one gain understanding of "the real universe?"

1、 Always understand that there is always more
   happening than what you think you see
2、 Focus on the edge and what's behind any object or
   phenomenon
3、 Heighten senses beyond sight, especially sound
4、 Witness impermanence in the immediate experience
5、 Feel the energy of your surrounding environment
6、 Immerse yourself in nature

WDIKN:
Every moment/experience is vibrant … stay alert.

THE TEN DEDICATIONS

Benefactor Twenty-One
Utpalabhuti "The Perfumer"

Male Layman

"A perfumer symbolizes the combining of knowledge and compassion, noumenon and phenomena, nirvana and samsara, and the ideas of defilement and purity all into one ball while still freely totalizing or distinguishing them?"

"The nature of fragrance rests on nothing, yet it radiates good and extinguishes bad; this symbolizes great vows that rely on nothing yet radiate deeds that benefit beings."

How does one practice, "great vows that rely on nothing?"

1、 "Great vows that rely on nothing" … means not relying on external conditions

2、 Cultivate true faith in what you know is true to sustain your vows

3、 Start with small vows and make them great by maintaining them until they are effortless

4、 Don't leak

5、 Practice right speech

6、 Pay the deepest attention to others of which you are capable

WDIKN:
This is the path to no regrets.

Benefactor Twenty-Two
Vaira "Independent"

Male Layman - Indestructible Dedication

Being profoundly calm and unshakable within the ocean of birth and death.

1、 See birth and death as natural by witnessing them both within each moment

2、 Live with awareness of impermanence and it's resultant uncertainty

3、 Uncertainty breeds anxiety and from it issues the fear of death

4、 When you really see the nature of this life, it's laughable

5、 Search for the deepest truths within yourself

6、 Don't die before you ever let yourself be here

WDYKN:
I must stand firm on what I know is true and be steadfast to disarm what stops me.

Benefactor Twenty-Three
Jayottama "Supreme Victor"

Male Layman - Dedication equal to all Buddhas
Supremacy of patience establishes the mind as spacious and whole

Fostering the power of pure faith in them (the Buddhas)

1、 Faith is not blind, blind faith is just belief

2、 Faith is based on knowing

3、 Faith is what keeps us connected to our knowing

4、 It sustains us beyond the distractions of the world

5、 Hold fast to your own experience in dark times

6、 Create personal rituals of devotion to connect with the inner truth of your own knowing

WDIKN:
The times are dark. I must work diligently not to succumb to hopelessness. Cultivate gratitude. See perfection and beauty in the smallest of acts.

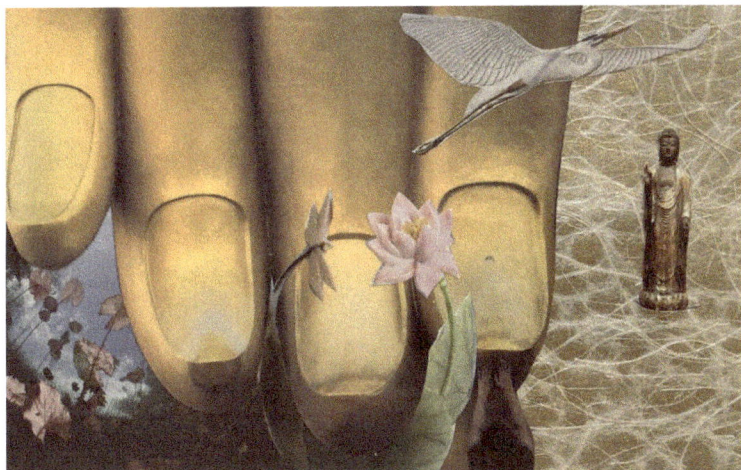

Benefactor Twenty-Four
Sinhavijurmbhita – "Lion Stretch"

Female Nun
Realizing dedication reaching all places

A doctrine called resorting to the treasury of one's own mind.

1、 "One's own mind" is vast and boundless

2、 Limited by the attachment of conditioned states

3、 Inherited from past ages, both aspects, positive and negative

4、 "Treasury" is the potential for awakening the unsurpassable mind

5、 Patience of the ages will be required

6、 Witness each moment in the vastness of no-time

WDIKN:
Cultivate a reverent manner. Understand the dharma of every experience.

Benefactor Twenty-Five
Vasumitra "Friend of the World"

Female Teacher
"Those who have heard my teaching and attain dispassion achieve an enlightening concentration called 'realm of nonattachment.'

I would like to understand what is meant by "realm of nonattachment."

1、 "Realm" means special knowing that endures

2、 Trade opinion for discernment

3、 Discernment is seeing without judgment

4、 Change with ease through the power of knowing

5、 View relative reality as a metaphor

6、 Maintain the attention necessary to live at the depth of metaphor

WDIKN:
Vasumitra's teaching, as all the others, offer guidance for maintaining presence. Cultivate dignity.

Benefactor Twenty-Six
Veshthila "Embracer"

Male Layman – Stabilizes all roots of goodness

Because no beginning or end of the universe can be located, the vastness of knowledge and compassion has no boundaries.

1、 Knowledge and compassion are intimate with the limitlessness of the universe

2、 There can be no limits to what we need to know [understand]

3、 There is nothing for which we should not find compassion

4、 The mind quakes at the notion, and the heart weeps

5、 By what means can this be achieved?

6、 Taking refuge in the Buddha

WDIKN:
No matter how dark the circumstance internally or externally, listen deeply for, and trust, the pure voice of your own buddha-nature.

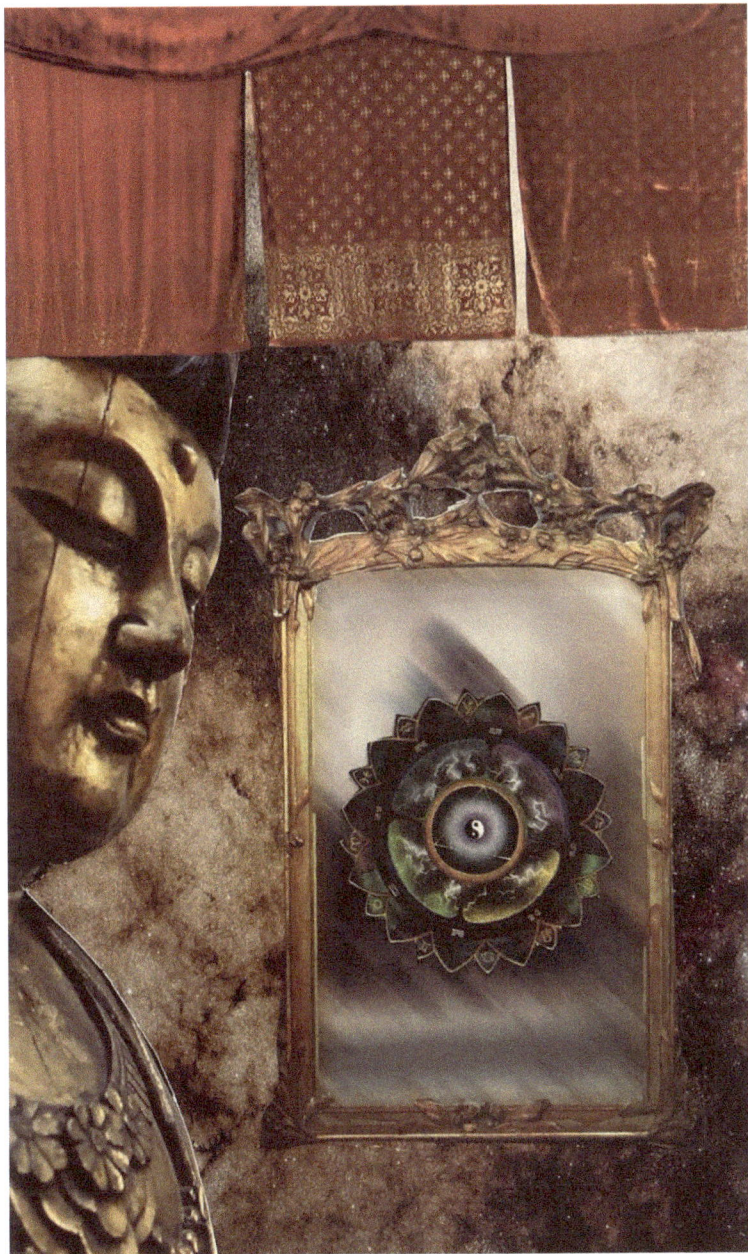

Benefactor Twenty-Seven
Avalokiteshvara "Acting in accord with the needs of all beings"

Male Enlightening Being

"Any who remember my name go without fear ...
No harm will come to them, but rather benefit instead,
If they remember my name, even for a while. ...
Those who remember my name will gain release."

1、 I can't imagine it

2、 It is what must be achieved

3、 "When the mind is no hindrance, no fears exist"

4、 Heal the mind stream of grief

5、 Don't be afraid of the dark places within

6、 Truly understand that you are enough as you are

WDIKN:
Just begin though the task is endless

Benefactor Twenty-Eight
Ananyagamin "He Who Proceeds Directly"

Male Enlightening Being – True Thusness opens the world of the Buddhas

What does it mean to "honor each Buddha with the finest mentally produced offerings"?

1、 See "each" thing in your world as a Buddha

2、 Recognize what those in your opinion are negative and difficult to see as Buddhas have to offer

3、 Hold fast to the teachings you have learned

4、 See each moment [action] within the vastness of space and time

5、 Respond immediately to any generous impulse

6、 Release yourself quickly of negative responses to others, things, or situations

WDYKN:
Pure intention is what constitutes the "finest mentally produced offerings."

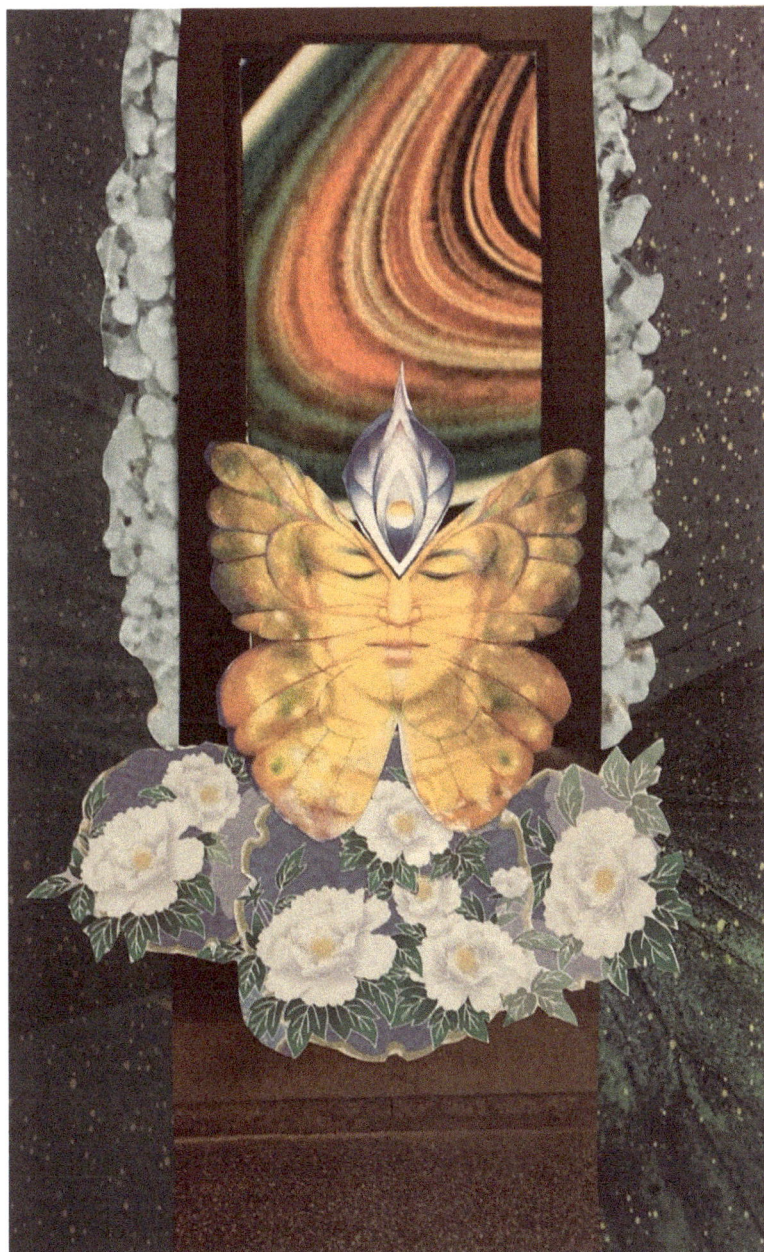

Benefactor Twenty-Nine
Mahadeva "The Great God"

Male Celestial – Mahadeva "attained 'cloud net' liberation, showering teaching as rain from clouds of great compassion and rescuing sentient beings as with a net."

Mahadeva lived at Dvaravati, which means, "Having a Door." How should I understand that, "There is a great door of truth that opens up to enlighten sentient beings."

1、 The door opens from the inside

2、 Fear and Doubt are the locks on the door

3、 Understand there is no external refuge

4、 Cultivate fearlessness in pursuit of liberation

5、 Understand "reality" as a metaphor of a deeper truth

6、 Make yourself receptive to the help of the Buddhas

WDIKN:
Make your practice more devotional by cultivating personally meaningful rituals.

Benefactor Thirty
Sthavara "Stable"

Female Earth Goddess – Represents the substance of great compassion, always functioning yet always tranquil. This is why she is called Stable.

*Infinite dedication equal to the cosmos frees one
from the yoke of the scarcity of time.*

1、 Time is equal to the vastness of the Universe

2、 We live within many timeframes

3、 Personal, universal, cosmic

4、 The true place to reside is the "timeless" realm

5、 Witness, there, the speed and transformation of interdependence

6、 Act in the world with that understanding at the base

WDIKN:
Becoming "stable" is an act of understanding, remembering, and embracing vastness and timelessness.

Dancing with the Benefactors

Benefactor Thirty-One
Vasanti – "Joyousness"

Female Goddess - Joyousness is the natural expression that
arises when fear is dispelled.

How can one be free from the "fear of darkness"?

1、 Darkness encompasses the many things we fear.

2、 Correct fear serves to protect

3、 Most fears are imagined

4、 Distinguish the fear that serves from the fears
that are imagined

5、 Know the difference in your body.

6、 Imagined fears are confusion and chaos resulting
in anxiety.

7、 Fears that serve are alert, calm, and informative.

WDIKN:
It is helpful to remember that the times when I really was in
danger there wasn't time to be afraid, but was alert, thought
clearly, and discerned a course of action.

Benefactor Thirty-Two
Samamtagambhirashrivimalaprabha
Site of Enlightenment – "Purity"

Female Night Goddess – Her purity is rooted in her mind's focus on the salvation and protection of living beings.

"To realize the purity of inherent nature of all beings with equanimity, detached from the mundane world."

1、 Equanimity detached from the mundane world is seeing without judgment and opinion.

2、 Without judgment and opinion, one must still discern what is good from what is harmful.

3、 Situations are fluid, one must reassess continuity.

4、 Purity of inherent nature is obscured by mistaken actions due to misunderstanding.

5、 All beings are part of the mundane world.

6、 It cannot be abandoned.

WDIKN:
To see beyond the limits of the mundane world one must stand unperturbed within unknowing without detachment to what is happening.

Benefactor Thirty-Three
Collage I
Joyful Eyes Illuminating - "Refulgence"

Female Night Goddess - The practice of great compassion is not limited by time.

"The radiant mind of refulgence is the all-encompassing mind of Buddha-nature."

1、 All-encompassing means without limits.

2、 Mind without limits.

3、 Buddha-nature is all that is.

4、 Understanding interdependence is the womb of compassion.

5、 Trust in Buddha-nature renders confidence to act without needing to be understood.

6、 It is enough to be aligned with one's purest intention.

WDIKN:
Do not hesitate to express caring. It demonstrates faith in one's own Buddha-nature.

Dancing with the Benefactors

Benefactor Thirty-Three
Collage II
Joyful Eyes Illumining the World — Refulgence

Female Night Goddess – The radiance of refulgence represents the initiating action of enlightenment that works directly in cultivating protection and increased well-being of all beings.

"The Personal and Universal Minds act in unending concordance in creating compassion for self and others."

1、 The personal mind is dependent on Universal Mind for the wisdom to know Right View and Right Action

2、 It is the task of discriminating mind [personal mind] to learn how to dialogue with Universal Mind

3、 Trusting intuition is the kay

4、 One needs to overcome doubt and trust their own experience

5、 One must develop forgiveness for self and others

6、 Forgiveness is the path for cultivating compassion

WDIKN:
Forgiveness is understanding and acceptance that frees oneself from entanglement with the sources of pain. It includes clarity for appropriate response from the source of such pain. Neither wound what was wounded you nor allow continued pain from that source.

BACKGROUND
MATERIAL

EMERGENT
KNOWLEDGE

"Between the Universal Mind and the Personal Mind
is the intuitive-mind, which is dependent upon Universal Mind
for its cause and support and enters into relation with both.
It partakes of the universality of Universal Mind,
and shares its purity.
Through the intuitive-mind, the faculty of intuition,
the inconceivable wisdom of Universal Mind is revealed
and made realizable."
Shakyamuni Buddha in the Lankavatara Sutra

Note to Reader

Familiarity with *Tending the Fire: An Introspective Guide to Zen Awakening* and the basic Yogacara teachings are helpful for understanding the objective of this work.

Introduction to Emergent Knowledge

"Human life on earth is conditioned and unfree,
and when people recognize this limitation
and make themselves dependent upon
the harmonious and beneficent forces of the cosmos,
they achieve success."[6]
I Ching Hexagram #30 Li, The Clinging Fire

In July 1975, we headed out of California with years of experience to sort through. We sat in a Coalville, Utah restaurant one morning engaged in our never-ending conversation on Zen practice and teaching methods. Zen found the shores of the West only a few years before, and our interest was even fresher. We discussed how prospects at the beginning of a movement are open to creative forms and innovative ideas. As we ate our eggs and toast, we dreamed of establishing a lay order free of hierarchy, guided by consensus, with emphasis on shared study. Zen practice would bring us together and provide the basis and power for mutual awakening. Over the years we maintained enthusiasm in the face of many unknowns and setbacks.

Our marriage was only possible because we had both understood individually that living committed to the process of awakening was our way of life. Soon after meeting, we understood this about each other. We became engaged and were married within two months. Our life together was fun and exciting in a reflective and reserved manner – and we did cultivate and pursue the process of awakening, meeting and studying with great teachers, and taking what we learned and putting it into action in various means, appropriate for the time and place. We produced a number of books, training, manuals, and all sorts of other activities and devices, in our attempt to communicate the importance of the process of awakening, and how others may awaken it in their lives.

However, the critical piece was the writing of the *Enhanced Emergent Knowledge* booklet. In October 2023 we wrote it and recognized it as the culmination of our fifty years together. In it, we communicated a practical response to Buddha's affirmation, "I have taught one thing and one thing only, *dukkha* and the cessation of *dukkha*." Shortly after its completion, Renshin's cancer metastasized and she succumbed in March 2024.

Much of the inspirational spark underlying this process resulted from Renshin's relationship with the innovative psycho-linguistic therapist, David Grove. He developed Clean Language, Metaphor Therapy, and eventually Emergent Knowledge.

Renshin attended his seminar in 1989 on Metaphor Therapy where she immediately recognized similarities between the methods of Zen practice and his Metaphor Therapy. She noted that Grove's approach offered a means beyond the limitations of cognitive understanding and coping with an identified problem. She understood that successful implementation of Metaphor Therapy, like Zen practice, resolved the root cause of conditioned states, liberating the individual from the afflictive pains and mental confusion associated with them. She learned Metaphor Therapy and applied it in her psychotherapy practice with promising results, prompting her to adapt it as a skillful means for Zen practice that she named Metaphor Awareness.

Both Metaphor Therapy and Metaphor Awareness are facilitator-based techniques requiring a high level of expertise on the part of the facilitator and substantial preparation time for the client/practitioner. Later, Grove developed a process called Emergent Knowledge that could be successfully accomplished without a facilitator, while staying true to his basic premises. This process offers a skillful means that practitioners can easily learn and creatively employ. We combined Emergent Knowledge with Zen practice, yielding a process that contains the means to access and develop the transformative power of Buddhist awakening.

Subsequently, elements of these methods were taken up and over a thirty-five-year period, tested and adapted by Renshin, and formed into *Enhanced Emergent Knowledge*. It was "Enhanced" because it contained two Yogacara Buddhist elements added to Grove's unidimensional approach. Its use offers an opportunity to activate and manifest the process of awakening. The central importance of the intuitional activity of inquiry and response was explained without using Buddhist terminology or psychological explanations. The booklet describes the essence of Buddhist wisdom – prajna, intuition – without ever mentioning it, compiling in secular terms our experience that arose from our studies and practice. Anyone can follow the directions and resolve an identified problem, transform it into a pathway of freedom, and then live the changes and arrive at balance and freedom in their lives. Both *Enhanced Emergent Knowledge* and *Emergent Knowledge and Zen Practice* versions are offered below.[7]

We followed a long, circuitous path in assembling the *Enhanced Emergent Knowledge* instruction booklet. But completing it, we felt we had succeeded in being able to communicate our life experience, surrounding the study of the process of awakening with meaningful and coherent facts. I say "we" because I played a part. But it is Renshin's creative insights that form its heart. She stayed true to her life's vocation, freely presenting her wisdom for anyone who would wish to follow her innovative path.

Enhanced Emergent Knowledge

Renshin and Taizen Verkuilen
10/10/2023

Enhanced Emergent Knowledge

[The] key to personal transformation: my life situation can be transformed by reforming what motivates my actions right now, and by making these volitions habitual.[8]

I. WHAT IS EMERGENT KNOWLEDGE?

Emergent Knowledge is an introspective method of studying the self that relies solely on an individual's insight, intuition, and tacit knowledge. The skills required for successful application of Emergent Knowledge are clarity of intention and nonjudgmental attention. Emergent Knowledge offers unlimited potential for beneficial change, subtle and profound. Its systematic approach provides an accessible means to move from coping with afflictive emotions to freedom from them, achieved through the process of transformation. By means of an explicit system of investigation, intuitive information arises and gives form and clarity to a practitioner's problem and its resolution. Generating, developing, and integrating this information need not be a mystery or left to happenstance.

Emergent Knowledge is a psycho-linguistic method of questioning an individual's inner life, accessing information uncontaminated by interpretation from either a facilitator or practitioner. This form of inquiry enables intimate dialogue free of interjections and presuppositions. The pioneering psychotherapist David Grove developed it. He discovered that questions that least interfered with a client's experience were in fact the most effective in bringing about meaningful change.

Emergent Knowledge is a user-based method of investigation that neither taints nor distorts information that arises during inquiry, by applying a limited number of precisely worded questions. The process allows facilitators and practitioners to refrain from unconsciously projecting into their experience unresolved issues and interpretations.

Grove's first developments were Metaphor Therapy and Cosmology of Space, but later their essential elements were adapted for the facilitator-free process of Emergent Knowledge. Emergent Knowledge provides a systematic method that can be, after initial training, successfully accomplished without a facilitator. This technique is easy to learn and apply, offering a means to address varied problematic issues. The goal of Emergent Knowledge is to resolve negative dynamics that are repetitive, and that limits one's ability to respond to life situations as one might otherwise prefer.

Emergent Knowledge's precise rules of questioning are a simple reproducible information-centered approach that:

- Helps to foster a state of concentration necessary to observe the response without recourse to analysis or reflection
- Avoids contamination by unnecessary interpretations
- Resonates with the practitioner's unique autonomous healing and learning process

II. THE PURPOSE, FORM, AND METHOD OF EMERGENT KNOWLEDGE

How to Begin

You may use Emergent Knowledge for any problem you might wish to resolve, goal you'd like to achieve, or decision you need to make.

It is best to work with a pencil and paper, as the information is ephemeral and slips away like a dream when we awake from sleep. Begin where you are. Set the intention of the session by asking and answering:

"What do you want?" The outcome will be a "Want Statement."

For Example: *I want to be able to study without anxiety.*

Repeat the statement three times, silently or out loud. The question series should be done quickly without analysis, even though some responses may not make sense. These actions hone intuitive receptiveness and trust in the process.

[1] Now ask yourself: What is the first thing I know about that? Record the response.
[2] And what else? Record response.
[3] And what else? Record response.
[4] And what else? Record response.
[5] And what else? Record response.
[6] And what else? Record response.
[7] And what do I know now that I didn't know before? [WDIKN?] Record response.

The answer to WDIKN is known as the "Proclamation Statement."

It is important not to reject or second-guess the responses that comes up, even if you don't understand them. There is time to reflect on the answers after the session is completed.

Below are three individual's records. The first deals with an outer relationship, the second with an internal emotional concern, and third for deepening insight.

"Nancy"
Want Statement: *I want to get along with my co-worker Jim.*

[1] What is the first thing you know about that? *He makes me defensive.*
[2] And what else? *I'm anxious.*
[3] And what else? *I freeze.*
[4] And what else? *He is brash to everyone.*
[5] And what else? *It isn't just about me.*
[6] And what else? *It's about who he is.*
[7] And what do I know now that I didn't know before?

Proclamation Statement:
I don't have to like him to work with him. All I have to do is to remember this.

"Bob"
Want Statement: *I want be less anxious about the future.*

[1] What is the first thing you know about that? *I am always anxious.*
[2] And what else? *I'm like my father.*
[3] And what else? *It's tiring and it doesn't help.*
[4] And what else? *I can't know outcomes.*
[5] And what else? *Just do the best I can.*
[6] And what else? *I need to trust myself.*
[7] And what do I know now that I didn't know before?

Proclamation Statement:
The only thing I can really do is to take care of whatever situation I'm in, the best I can.

In addition to Emergent Knowledge being used for problem resolution, it can be applied beneficially for gaining insight and deepening understanding. Below is an example.

"Jean"

Want Statement: *I want to understand the meaning of autonomy more deeply.*

[1] What do I know about autonomy? *It's my relationship to myself.*
[2] And what else? *It means staying centered in my relationship to the world.*
[3] And what else? *I lose connection with it when I worry about what others think.*
[4] And what else? *I'm ineffective when that occurs.*
[5] And what else? *I need to recognize that more quickly.*
[6] And what else: *See what actions I must take to regain balance and the proper relationship to the world.*
[7] And what do I know now that I didn't know before?

Proclamation Statement:
My sense of autonomy is dependent on the level of awareness I maintain in my interactions with the world.

The responses to the examples above may seem questionable to you, but they were intimate glimpses for Nancy, Bob, and Jean for their own understanding. The answers are always idiosyn-cratic. Your work only has to be meaningful to you. When it is, you may change and your relationship to the world can change.

A few weeks after their Emergent Knowledge session, Nancy, Bob, and Jean were asked to write a brief report on any changes they may have experienced.

Nancy Reported:

"I didn't notice any change for the first couple of days back to work. Then I read again the Post Emergent Knowledge Session Process (*outlined below*) and found it very helpful. When I said I didn't see any changes, there actually were some. The "habit energies" confused me. Then I noticed that I was able to stay steady when they did arise. What I mean by that is, I felt less defensive in his presence even though my stomach still tightened when first encountering him. Knowing that I was able to get past the discomforting feelings, I could think beyond them. What I mean by that is I could be more present in the circumstance, not freeze. The habit energies slowly ebbed to nothing. Also, I was more able to observe how other co-workers react to him. It was obvious many have ill feelings toward Jim. That actually made me feel sorry for him. Anyway, in just over a month or so, the situation is really different in ways I never thought could be possible. I feel more relaxed at work. I actually don't dislike him, although he can still be irritating. We are not friends outside the office, but feel I am better able to get along with him as a co-worker."

Bob Reported:

"I feel more relaxed in my body, even when thinking about the future.

110

I can have thoughts about the future without feeling overwhelmed.

I don't just start imagining crises all the time.

I feel more comfortable with the unknown when thinking about the future.

I feel more engaged with my life as it is now.

Over all, I do feel less anxious. All I can say about that is, Wow!"

Jean Reported:

In the weeks since my Emergent Knowledge session on Autonomy, I've noticed feeling more confident in social encounters. This was true even in instances of meeting new people, which always made me more nervous than I thought I should be feeling. I guess I'm just more confident in myself. I find I'm much less concerned about what others think of me. It's not that I don't care. It's just that I'm not preoccupied by that. This feels significant to me.

When working with the process, you may find that the first three responses may come quite easily. The information is not surprising or particularly inspiring. For the most part, it tends to be what we cognitively already know. At step 4 (what David Grove called "the wobble"), there may be a pause before the next response. It is easy to feel that there is no more information available. Hold your nonjudgmental awareness and wait patiently for the response to come. It will. Steps 4, 5, and 6 present the information that offers deeper understanding.

It is essential not to reflect on responses until after Step 7 is completed. In Steps 1—7, reflections will inhibit the smooth flow of the process. The information derived at Step 7 can be used as the "Want Statement" of another Emergent Knowledge round of inquiry, if you intuitively feel the round is incomplete. The deeper you drill down with a series of inquiries, the more meaningful the understanding and subsequent change. When doing more than one round, use the meaning of Proclamation Statement to form the Want Statement of the next round. "Six rounds" is called a series and usually leads to in-depth under-standing and change.

The more you work with Emergent Knowledge the easier it will flow, but Step 4 will usually to be a turning point.

Post Emergent Knowledge Session Process

Emergent Knowledge requires observational skills after a session. The changes need to be noted to gain the full benefit of the process, especially soon after a session is completed. The dynamics we may choose to work on can have long-standing tendencies that frustrate us. There tends to be an energy to their arising that is automatic that doesn't disappear immediately after working on it. These are called "habit energies." It takes keen attention to note the differences. This is difficult because we are used to the dynamic arising and may mistakenly assume the session was unproductive. Attention is needed to notice the subtle difference in our responses.

When it is just the 'habit energy' we find that their arising does not elicit our habitual response to it. It doesn't go to the same place in us. We do not get upset in the usual way. Becoming aware when the now distraction-only habit energies occur, observing them and dismissing them, aids in ending their appearance.

The stages to work and observe after Proclamation are:

Discerning Differences – There can be an odd sensation of disorientation, that is not unpleasant. It feels curious to be free of the afflictive energy of the problem. Yet, the change is not articulated specifically. It may feel vague and amorphous.

Clarifying Details – We can name and identify how the differences manifest. The residue of the resolved problem is more easily dealt with. Freedom from it becomes the new way of sensing the self.

Acceptance – Requires enough time living the changes to accept they are enduring. One can fully grasp the significance of the transition from the problematic symptom.

Relief & Comfort – Issues forth a recognition of a change of behavior. To be free from the habit energy of the dynamic worked on brings a sense of relief and gratitude.

Naturalness – Living without the discomfort of the original dynamic, sometimes finding it to be difficult to even remember the problem. One can live freed from the boundary of limitations the dynamic created. Naturalness is activated awareness, with unencumbered activity as the outcome.

A PRACTICE EMERGENT KNOWLEDGE SESSION
Create a Want Statement [a statement of intention]

[1] What is the first thing I know about that? Record response.

[2] And what else? Record response.

[3] And what else? Record response.

[4] And what else? Record response.

[5] And what else? Record response.

[6] And what else? Record response.

[7] WHAT DO I KNOW NOW THAT I DIDN'T KNOW
     BEFORE? [WDIKN] [PROCLAMATION STATEMENT]
     RECORD RESPONSE.

III. DOCUMENTATION OF EMERGENT KNOWLEDGE

All information connected with the Emergent Knowledge session should be documented using the Emergent Knowledge Documentation sheet. Practitioners should carry a notebook so that thoughts and reflections that arise can be recorded and later transferred to the documentation sheet.

I. The required information includes:

1、 An identified, observed, and studied problem.

2、 A Want Statement (s) based on the problem (or a WDIKN responses in multiple round sessions)

3、 Response to each of the six questions

4、 Answer(s) to a WDIKN question(s)

5、 All intuitions, reflections, and inferences that arise during and after formation of the Proclamation Statement

II. Recording Information

1、 Enter information about the problem to be used in the top row boxes.

2、 Formulate a Want Statement based on the problem and enter in Round 1 "Want Statement."

3、 Record each response.

4、 Enter Round 1 answer to WDIKN. If this is the completion of the session, enter the WDIKN answer in Proclamation.

5、 For multiple round sessions, formulate a Want Statement using the previous Round's WDIKN. Then repeat items 3 and 4.

6、 For multiple round sessions, the Proclamation Statement is the last WDIKN.

Documenting captures ephemeral insights and provides the framework for gauging progress, introspection, and in time, reveals hidden relationships. The thoroughness and accuracy of the documentation of information determines the depth and speed of the assimilation of benefits from the session.

EMERGENT KNOWLEDGE DOCUMENTATION

What is the problem??	How does the problem affect me?	What triggers the problem?			
Round 1 Want Statement	Round 2 Want Statement	Round 3 Want Statement	Round 4 Want Statement	Round 5 Want Statement	Round 6 Want Statement
1					
2					
3					
4					
5					
6					
WDIKN	WDIKN	WDIKN	WDIKN	WDIKN	WDIKN
Proclamation	Discerning Differences	Clarifying Details	Acceptance	Relief and Comfort	Naturalness

IV. IMPORTANT POINTS IN EMERGENT KNOWLEDGE

I. Before Emergent Knowledge Questioning

Cultivate a deep and wide understanding of all aspects of the problem that has your attention. Take time to thoroughly grasp the effects of the problem on your life, and only then formulate a Want Statement.

II. During Emergent Knowledge Questioning

Approach Emergent Knowledge sessions with a calm deliberate mind. Cultivate awareness of the intimate spot where the information arises. Ask the questions as described and record the responses without analysis or reflection. Upon completion of the six questions ask and answer the WDIKN question, and write out the Proclamation Statement for that round.

III. Major Points of Understanding after the Emergent Knowledge Session

David Grove's teaching on Emergent Knowledge ended at the writing of the Proclamation Statement. However, in Enhanced Emergent Knowledge, two additional sections have been devised that offer a means to refine the beneficial effects summarized in the Proclamation Statement. They are introspective methods that instruct practitioners to integrate the freedom that results from their resolution.

Each of the stages performs two services:
1. Summarizes the action and effects of the process.
2. Supplies direction for correct orientation. Each label is associated with an expansive introspection and a proper alignment with the process, providing

correct guidance in transformation of mental afflictions.

The first section offers a means to integrate the freedom gained from Emergent Knowledge questioning. It is a step-by-step method that directs how to reduce leftover habit energies, remnants of the problem identified in the Want Statement that may continue to arise.

ADDED SECTION 1 - INTEGRATING FREEDOM [BLUE ON DOCUMENTATION SHEET]

1、 Discerning Differences focuses on the comparison of the Want Statement to present emotional and intellectual circumstances, and to notice the presence, frequency, and intensity level of habit energies.

2、 Clarifying Details: Continues the work of Discerning Differences. The practitioner clearly articulates observed differences, appreciating and enjoying them.

3、 Acceptance: Acknowledges the enduring quality of the changes and weakening of habit energies.

4、 Relief and Comfort: Practitioners note that habit energies associated with the problem identified in the Want Statement do not arise.

ADDED SECTION 2 - LIVING FREEDOM [RED ON DOCUMENTATION SHEET]

1、 Naturalness: Living freely without memory or encumbrance of the problem described in the Want Statement. Unencumbered activity is the new normal state of affairs.

V. RECURRING THEMES IN EMERGENT KNOWLEDGE

Attributes of Emergent Knowledge

1、 Provides the foundation for identifying problems that cause emotional affliction and/or mental confusion.

2、 Provides the means to clarify the source of environmental triggers of identified problems.

3、 The six questions bring the practitioner to a transformation and a psychophysical shift that uproots the problem.

4、 Provides an initial awakening that presents the pathway to freedom.

5、 The Proclamation Statement captures and summarizes the answers to the Emergent Knowledge six questions.

6、 The process gives equal value to rational inquiry and intuitive response.

7、 Prepares the practitioner for the integration of freedom and the creation of harmony of the Personal and Universal Aspects of Mind.

8、 Removal of obstruction provides a means of healing.

9、 With mature experience, the resolution process moves with increased speed.

Emergent Knowledge qualities to be developed and cultivated:

1、 Do it on your own: Practitioners should develop confidence in their own abilities.

2、 Develop a sense of composure: Practitioners should practice with unfaltering calm, not beset by confusion and worries. (*Don't be confused by the confusion.*)

3、 Be neither tense nor slack: Being tense impregnates the mind with anxiety; being slack opens the door to torpor.

4、 Do not seek a particular emotional feel: Awareness should proceed without requiring a particular "taste"; there is no value in adding or subtracting from an experience.

5、 Abandon efforts of only intellectual understanding: trust intuition and insights.

6、 Establish and cultivate a continuity of awareness: Fully engage with each inquiry and response.

7、 Understand, refine, and integrate the essence of the Proclamation Statement.

8、 Follow the process to completion: Understand and follow the five-fold elements of mental discipline, concentration, insight, liberation, and living freely.

Emergent Knowledge
and
Zen Practice

Renshin and Taizen Verkuilen
Original version: 10/2010
Revised 6/2018

INTRODUCTION TO EMERGENT KNOWLEDGE AND ZEN PRACTICE

The synthesis of Emergent Knowledge and Zen practice grew out of Renshin's insight into Metaphor Therapy. Two sections of Yogacara teachings – refinement and integration of Thusness and living freely – were added to Grove's original conception to complete the adaptation of Emergent Knowledge for Zen practitioners. These additions changed Emergent Knowledge into a process of inquiry-response dialogue closely matching Zen's traditional teaching means.

The following seven sections will explore how the methods of Emergent Knowledge are similar to Zen's traditional process of awakening, review the background principles of Emergent Knowledge, and describe how to apply and document its practice.

Section 1 Observing the Critical Phrase: Master Ta-hui' s "Short-cut" Method of Koan Introspection

This section offers a description of Ta-hui Tsung-kao's [1089-1163] traditional koan introspection called "observing the critical phrase" [k'an-hua Chinese]. His adaptation of early koan introspection methods rekindled Rinzai Zen practice with an originality that continues into the present time. Learning Ta-hui's shortcut method removes unnecessary efforts from the process of awakening, focusing practitioners' minds on what is essential. This recounting of the rejuvenation of 12th century Rinzai Zen is included because of the many equivalencies it has with Emergent Knowledge and our modern circumstances.

Section 2 A Description of Emergent Knowledge
The principles of Emergent Knowledge as formulated by David Grove are described along with the basic method of application used in psychotherapy practice. Additions will be made in later chapters that combine it with the Zen process of awakening.

Section 3 Commonalities and Contrasts between Observing the Critical Phrase and Emergent Knowledge
The common areas of Master Ta-hui's "shortcut" method and Zen adapted Emergent Knowledge are compared and studied as to how their distinct methodologies arrive at the same objective of awakening.

Section 4 The Three Sources of Knowledge: Guiding Principles of Zen Practice
Chinese Zen Master Tsung-mi recounts how the Indian masters of Buddhism declared that Zen practice requires three sources of knowledge – the sutras, the unmediated direct perception of Zazen, and wide-ranging inferential reasoning and introspection. All three are necessary to ensure success in understanding and applying the process of awakening.

Section 5 The Nonduality – Resolution Sequence Symbol
The Nonduality – Resolution Sequence Symbol consolidates and expresses in graphical form Tsung-mi's three sources of knowledge. It can be used with any method of Zen practice because the symbol is a universal representation of the process of awakening.

Section 6 The Emergent Knowledge Summary Symbol
The Emergent Knowledge / Nonduality – Resolution Sequence
Symbol offers a one-page sheet that summarizes the application
of Emergent Knowledge. It is a map that contains the principles
of Yogacara Buddhism and the Resolution Sequence along with
basic directions to implement Emergent Knowledge's method
of inquiry.

SECTION 7 Documentation of Emergent Knowledge

* * * * * * * *

The 21st-century innovation of Emergent Knowledge has
similar features of Ta-hui's 12th-century modifications of koan
practice. They both promise a short-cut method to access
awakening through an all-inclusive systematic process.
Knowledge of Ta-hui's originality in responding to the creative
needs of his time provides helpful guidance and perspective for
devising a 21st century skillful means. Section 1 will review
Ta-hui's work before Section 2 offers an accounting of
Emergent Knowledge.

Section 1
Observing the Critical Phrase:
Master Ta-hui's "Short-cut" Method of
Koan Introspection

"Thousands and ten-thousands of times during the twenty-four hours of the day, don't allow yourself to waste time: day by day, in your daily venue of activities, know you are complete and radiant and not the least different from Shakyamuni and Bodhidharma."[10]
—Zen Master Ta-hui

Nine hundred years ago, an old Chinese Zen monk decided to retire to his hometown to spend his last years. Despite his best efforts he had been unable to achieve the goals he set for himself in his youth, leaving him dissatisfied. Just before he left the monastery, a turn of luck came his way. A young colleague counseled him to make one final try with Master Ta-hui who taught a newly improvised short-cut form of koan introspection. The old monk took his advice, sought out and accepted Ta-hui's teaching. This time the old monk's efforts had an effective tool. Ta-hui's short-cut method opened access to sudden awakening and profound realization.

The use of koan introspection became wide spread during the Chinese Sung Dynasty [960-1279]. Teachers of the 10th and 11th centuries compiled collections of stories of the great Zen masters of the T'ang dynasty using them to highlight essential Zen teachings. Each koan depicts a Zen Master's enlightened mind, and is a guide capable of bringing a student to awakening. Scholars suggest two reasons that brought about

127

the formulation and growth of the various forms of koan introspection during Sung Dynasty:

- To provide skillful means appropriate for the needs of the students of that time
- Methods of koan introspection were a natural development out of the creative flowering of Sung Dynasty Zen practice.

Ta-hui was a 12th-century Chinese Zen master, a Dharma holder of the Lin-chi school. He was instrumental in adapting the use of the koan collections, moving their use away from emphasis on discussion and discursive thinking. Ta-hui insisted that the koan's purpose was "to open the eyes of the patch-robed monks of the world," not to act as a literary agent or puzzle.[11] Observing the critical phrase refuted intellectual understanding as the pinnacle of practice, thus supporting its removal as an obstacle to awakening. To resolve the critical phrase Ta-hui advised,

> *"If you want to understand the principle of the short-cut, you must in one fell swoop break through this one thought – then and only then will you comprehend birth and death. Then and only then will it will be called accessing awakening…You need only to lay down, all at once, the mind full of deluded thoughts and inverted thinking, the mind of logical discrimination, the mind that loves life and hates death, the mind of knowledge and views, interpretation and comprehension, and the mind that rejoices in stillness and turns from disturbance."* [12]

Only the critical phrase and the direct path to awakening are left after jettisoning the unneeded reflections, mental habits, and deluded thoughts.

Ta-hui trained practitioners to focus on the principal topic or most essential element of the koan case. He declared observing the critical phrase a short-cut leading to sudden awakening. This form of observation identified and centered introspection on the critical phrase rather than attempting to grasp the entire koan at once. Observing the critical phrase helped keep attention on the immediate moment, locked into the unfolding of the immediate moment. Koan introspection emerged following Ta-hui's creative alteration as a honed contemplative tool for realizing our innate ability to awaken.

Ta-hui recognized ordinary life as the ideal venue for the practice of observing the critical phrase. He taught that observing the critical phrase is best practiced amid the typical responsibilities, encounters, uncertainties, and afflictions of ordinary life. Monastery life offers a controlled lifestyle exempt from the cares of family, employment, and earning a living. A layperson's place in the world furnishes learning opportunities a monk's life cannot provide. Lay practitioners who adopt observing the critical phrase recognize its transformative nature as well as its ability to remove barriers to intuitive insight. The critical phrase consists of "live words" that leads to awakening, in contrast to "dead words" that lead only to intellectual understanding. Repeated introspection of the critical phrase catalyzes awareness of awakening enabling the growth of the accompanying liberating tension of "doubt." The force of doubt intensifies samadhi insight to the degree that ultimately brings about the realization of Thusness.

Ta-hui taught the way of the critical phrase as a deliberate and diligent engagement with the process of awakening rather than an attempt to "storm the ramparts." Sudden awakening shows up in an instant, but subsequent gradual cultivation penetrates the body and mind, slowly developing the nascent Thusness.

Section 2
A Description of Emergent Knowledge

"Don't ignore intuitive tickles
lest they reappear as sledgehammers."
Tenzing Norbu in Gay Hendricks'
The First Rule of Ten

Given the proven value of Ta-hui's observing the critical phrase, why do we need new ways to accomplish breakthrough? Many Sanghas use koans, but not all students benefit from that particular path of awakening. Practitioners, especially lay adherents, would greatly profit if another breakthrough alternative existed, a method that by intended design follows in exact harmony with a practitioner's particular path of awakening. Emergent Knowledge is like that; it is a process that begins with an identified conditioned state, followed by an unambiguous method that never deviates from a practitioner's immediate need.

Many contemporary Zen practitioners are in the same position of the old monk mentioned in the previous section; transformation eludes them despite their conscientious sincerity. Study and practice often times do not yield the full results they most earnestly seek. Like in Ta-hui's time, innovation is necessary. Our culture of college, family life, literacy, scientific education, and corporate employment necessitates adaptation of traditional teaching methods. These new forms must supply increased flexibility to cultivate the dynamic process of Zen Buddhist awakening for lay practitioners within their demanding fast-paced lives.

Emergent Knowledge is an introspective method of studying the self that relies solely on an individual's insight, intuition, tacit knowledge, and inherent purity. It is a process compatible with Zen study. The skills necessary for Zen practice are the same as those required for Emergent Knowledge: clarity of intention and nonjudgmental attention. Emergent Knowledge offers unlimited potential for beneficial change, both subtle and profound. Its systematic approach provides an accessible means to move from coping with afflictive emotions associated with conditioned states, to freedom from them achieved through the process of transformation. By means of an explicit system of investigation known as Clean Language, intuitive information arises and gives form and clarity to a practitioner's engagement with the process of awakening. Generating, developing, and integrating this information need not be a mystery or left to happenstance.

Clean Language is a psycho-linguistic method of questioning an individual's inner life, accessing information uncontaminated by interpretation from either the facilitator or practitioner. This form of inquiry enables intimate dialogue free of interjection of assumptions and presuppositions. The pioneering psychotherapist David Grove developed it in the 1980's. He discovered that questions that least interfered with a client's experience were in fact the most effective in bringing about meaningful change. Clean Language is a user-based method of investigation that neither taints nor distorts information arising during questioning. Grove subsequently fine-tuned Clean Language into a limited number of precisely worded questions for use with Emergent Knowledge. The process allowed the role of the facilitators and practitioners to stay "clean," and not unconsciously project their unresolved issues and interpretations.

.Clean Language was first used in Grove's Metaphor Therapy but later its essential elements were adapted for his facilitator-free process of Emergent Knowledge. Emergent Knowledge amended for Zen practice offers the means to approach problems or goals practitioners would like to resolve or achieve. Emergent Knowledge's "clean" precise rules of questioning are a simple reproducible information-centered approach that:

- Helps to foster a state of concentration necessary to observe the response without recourse to analysis
- Avoids contamination of the practitioner's experience
- Resonates with practitioner's experience
- Assists in the transformation of psychophysical imagery into words or the other way around
- Establishes and cultivates an open and intimate dialogue between the Personal and Universal Aspects of Mind

The typical Emergent Knowledge session contains these steps:

I. A conditioned state is identified and observed. Practitioners become familiar with what triggers it, as well as the thoughts, feelings, and reactive responses associated with it.[13]

It is essential to become thoroughly acquainted with the all aspects of the conditioned state. Becoming conversant with the way it manifests provides a firm foundation for clean questioning, and later aids when making "before and after" comparisons.

II. Formulation of a "Want Statement" based on awareness of the effects of a conditioned state or a spiritual issue.

The Want Statement is a "this moment" manifestation of a practitioner's Natural Koan. The Want Statement can take two forms:

- "I want to be free from…?" [a conditioned state that results in an afflictive emotion (*klesha*)]
- "I want to learn more about…?" [a desire for expanded knowledge about an insight]

Here are three examples:
I want to be free of nervousness in public speaking.
I want to understand spiritual authority.
I want to understand the meaning of autonomy more deeply.

III. Emergent Knowledge Questioning

Read the Want Statement slowly three times to focus attention. [The answers to the questions should be done without analysis. It is important not to reject or second-guess the response that comes up, even if you don't understand the response. There is time to reflect on the answers after the session is completed.]

1、 Now ask yourself: *What is the first thing I know about that?* Record the response.

2、 And what else? Record response.

3、 And what else? Record response.

4、 And what else? Record response.

5、 And what else? Record response.

6、 And what else? Record response.

7、 And what do I know now that I didn't know before? [WDIKN] Record response.

IV. The Proclamation Statement

The Proclamation Statement captures the information generated by the six questions, "proclaiming" the nature of the transformational change of being. The answer to the seventh question of "What do I know now that I did not know before? [WDIKN?] summarizes the changes effected by the six intuitional responses.

1、 The Proclamation Statement gives equal value to rational inquiry and the intuitive response.

2、 Its content is the foundation for the integration of freedom.

3. The Proclamation Statement defines the beginning of Reconstruction [the path of the Bodhisattva]

a. Refinement of commitment to the process of awakening

b. Eradication of leftover habit energies

c. Set the stage for naturalizing the creative interplay of the Personal and Universal Aspects of Mind.

4、 When mature practice is achieved, the resolution process moves with increased speed.

Section 3
Commonalities and Contrasts between Observing the Critical Phrase and Emergent Knowledge

"Effortless knowledge arises from the Universal Mind,
bestowed like a gift."
Flower Ornament Sutra

In Buddhist terms, the intent of Grove's method is almost identical to the first of the three legs of Yogacara Buddhism's process of awakening – resolving conditioned states. Emergent Knowledge was adapted for Zen practice by adding the second and third legs of integrating and living the freedom of Thusness. These additions expanded Grove's system resulting in a skillful means similar in function and outcome to Ta-hui's observing the critical phrase. The following describes their shared and contrasting features.

I. How the critical phrase and the Want Statement are applied

In observing the critical phrase, a fragment of a case is chosen that captures the heart of the story's meaning. The teacher chooses the case and critical phrase based on the disciple's need of the moment. For example, the Eleventh Case of the *Blue Cliff Record* – Huang Po's *Gobbler of Dregs* – states:

> *Huang Po, instructing the community said, "All of you*
> *are gobblers of dregs, if you go around this way where*
> *will you have Today? Do you know that there are no*
> *teachers of Ch'an in all of China?"*

At that time a monk came forward and said, "Then what about those in various places who order followers and lead communities?"
Huang Po said, I do not say there is no Ch'an; it's just that there are no teachers."[14]

In this example, the teacher may instruct the disciple to use "there are no teachers" as the critical phrase and the practitioner incorporates it into their daily practice. The phrase becomes the foundation of the thinking, reflection, analysis, and relationship, guiding the maturation of the disciple's spiritual vision. The teacher's role is to validate transformation but otherwise remain apart from judgment or interpretation.

In Emergent Knowledge, the practitioner writes a Want Statement that sets the intention of the session. The wording of the Want Statement contains the conditioned state and the desired outcome. The Want Statement is used to formulate the first Clean Language inquiry. For example: a Want Statement may be, *"I want to understand the meaning of autonomy more deeply."* The questioning of the session then goes on. After the session, the Want Statement and sense of change produced by the questioning are used as the foundations for the "before and after" comparisons.

Critical phrase introspection and Emergent Knowledge inquiry share the common feature of taking a small bite of the apple, not trying to swallow the whole apple at once. Ta-hui identifies one main topic of the koan and works with it; Emergent Knowledge singles out the conditioned state presently under observation and formulates the initiating Want Statement.

The assignment of the critical phrase and developing the Want Statement both recognize and cultivate the dawning of the Universal Aspect of Mind within the Personal Aspect. Traces of the Universal Mind are sought and found, verifying and expanding the understanding of the fecund relationship of the conditioned state (the mundane) and awakening (the sacred). This action is described as bringing the Universal to the Personal, the first and second awakenings. After sudden awakening, the Universal and Personal Aspects of Mind interact with fewer obstructions; this situation is described as bringing the Personal to the Universal, the third and fourth awakenings. Daily life attention with the critical phrase or Want Statement reveals their complementary transformative activity.

II. Repeated introspection of the critical phrase or questioning the Want Statement produces sudden awakening, the natural outcome of observation/inquiry.

Application of the methods of observing the critical phrase and the questioning of the Want Statement develops continuity of awareness. The Informal Mind of sitting (meditation in stillness) combined with the Formal Mind of right mindfulness (meditation in movement) helps to establish and cultivate a continuity of awareness in both areas.[15]

III. Both observing the critical phrase and Emergent Knowledge produce creative tension that undermines habitual rational processes.

A penetrating insight cuts through confusion, doubt, and insecurity, opening the road to the sought after sudden awakening. Confused states of mind are uprooted and the source and power of compulsive habits are identified and eliminated.

IV. Accessing and employing intuitive information uncontaminated by interpretation

In observing the critical phrase, the teacher assigns the case and phrase and then steps away allowing the disciple to find their own way, trusting in their inherent wisdom. This avoids corrupting the process with any attempt at helping with misguided interpretation.

In Emergent Knowledge practitioners define the Want Statement and ask the questions. This method remains pure and unadulterated if the practitioners maintain the unity of the inquiry-response process by not analyzing the intuitive non-conceptual information as it arises from within the Universal Aspect of Mind.

V. Ta-hui called the critical phrase a short-cut to sudden awakening. Emergent Knowledge quickly resolves conditioned states, its version of sudden awakening.

Both methods can be named short-cuts for a number of reasons, chief of which is cutting out the need for a lengthy and difficult education to acquire expertise in Buddhist concepts and practice techniques. Special knowledge and expertise are not necessary but can be learned and employed if so desired. Practitioners need only to learn the basics of sudden awakening by the use of the critical phrase and clean language questions, and cultivating them step-by-step after breakthrough.

VI. Kyogai — a demonstrable truth

And finally, there is kyogai, the way in which a koan affects your consciousness—in other words, the effect that it has on your life. This is ultimately where it counts. Because no matter how many hundreds of koans you pass through, if they do not change the way

you relate to the rest of the world, then they are nothing but intellectual exercises.
—John Daido Loori

What is Kyogai?

- Kyogai is the real-life affirmation of transformative change.
- Both observing the critical phrase and Emergent Knowledge remove karmic barriers to effecting and living the changes.

After removal of obstructions by the use of observing the critical phrase or Emergent Knowledge, practitioners realize these changes in their kyogai:

- Reduction of self-consciousness, capable of appropriately responding without hesitancy
- Has the ability to demonstrate understanding without resorting to explanations
- Growth in kyogai shows in fluency in behavior
- Kyogai means oneness with the incipient moment
- It is authentic activity itself, devoid of emotional bondage

Section 4
The Three Sources of Knowledge:
Guiding Principles of Zen Practice

"Indian Masters always held to three sources of knowledge.
Of the three, most Chan lineages have direct perception
and inference.
They must seal them with the third source, the sutras."[16]
—Zen Master Tsung-mi

The Indian Masters share the common assertion that three sources of knowledge are needed within Buddhist practice. Zen lineages generally teach Inference and Direct Perception, but often lack the anchoring experience of the Sutras. This situation is commonplace in Western Zen training facilities. Practitioners receive instruction in meditation techniques, but their efforts are often left ungrounded from the basic principles contained in the Sutras. The Three Sources must coincide in order for experience to be whole and complete. In other words, Inference and Direct Perception in meditation must be validated using the recognized standards of the Sutras. Then certainty arises becoming the foundation for subsequent insights by reducing the chance of erroneous conclusions.

The following simile of fire illustrates the nature of the three sources and the three ways we relate to them.

1、 First, a practitioner gains knowledge of fire – that is learning of the teachings, the authoritative Buddha's Word contained in the Sutras.

2、 Second, seeing smoke caused by the fire – infers the reality of teachings through the application of reason.

3、 Then, seeing the fire – experiencing the living reality of the teachings: Direct Perception.

What follows are brief descriptions of the three sources of knowledge:

I. The Sutras

The teachings of Shakyamuni Buddha were captured in the Sutras and preserved for our use. They are known as "Buddha's Word" because they express the authoritive explanations of the teachings. They serve as models by which to discern the false and correct. Some sutras express provisional teachings while others teach how to experience wisdom. We must rely on their complementary wholeness to understand the complete meaning of Buddha's teachings.

II. Inferential Introspection

Inferential thinking is reasoning in the form of deductions, inductions, conjectures, conclusions, speculation, reflection, logic, analysis, interpretation, explanation, and rationalization. Inferential thinking describes principles of the teachings, not the Dharma. Practitioners must be proficient in distinguishing principles and Dharma. Principles are products of conceptual thought; the Dharma arises from within non-conceptual knowing.

III. Direct Perception

Direct Perception is the phenomenal world [Personal] meeting true Dharma nature [Universal]. In Zen, practitioners are introduced and become familiar with this meeting in the practice of Zazen. In Zazen, practice and realization are one. Our body and mind attain balance and harmony with the correct application of the direct perception of Zazen. However, Master Tsung-mi cautions: "If one takes direct perception to be definitive by itself, and does not consult the sutras, how would that individual know how to anchor their experience to the true?"

Section 5
The Nonduality – Resolution sequence symbol

Without an outer teacher, the Resolution Sequence acts as an inner guide to minimize missteps and encourage diligence. [17]

Emergent Knowledge sessions can be conducted without knowledge of the Nonduality – Resolution Sequence Symbol, but using them together enhances the results of the introspective efforts and the accuracy of documentation.

The symbol titled "Nonduality – Resolution Sequence," graphically displays the process of dynamic change, the wholeness of being, and the wisdom of Nonduality. The purpose of the symbol is to provide support for the development of an individual undertaking Zen practice, and to act as a lifelong guide as one treads the path of awakening. The Nonduality – Resolution Sequence Symbol is like most other symbols; it encapsulates a broad understanding of many concepts and processes into a shorthand yet meaningful visual form. It is an invitation to the practitioner to invest energy in exploring and attaining a wide and deep mastery of Buddhist thought and experience.

Learning and employing the Nonduality – Resolution Sequence Symbol can help keep practitioners on track, even when a close relationship with a teacher is not at hand. The relationships contained within the symbol have the ability to paint a picture that is easily remembered and applicable to many varied internal and external life conditions. The symbol presents an opportunity to grasp the field of study as a whole, acting as a roadmap pointing the way, as well as providing a persistent stimulus against falling into naïve mental states. Resourceful introspection is an active contribution to the process of awakening.

The Three Sources of Knowledge of sutra teachings, direct perception, and inference are embedded in the process symbol.

I. Sutra guidance – symbolized Yogacara Teachings

The process of awakening is symbolized above. The symbol graphically displays the teachings of Yogacara Buddhism along

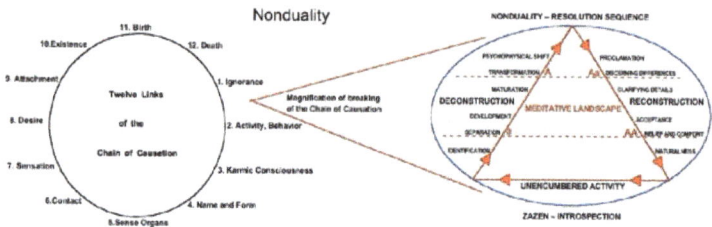

with the inferential introspection of the Resolution Sequence. Both Yogacara and the Resolution Sequence teach a means of transformation of consciousness based on accessing and employing intuitive information uncontaminated by interpretation by either the teacher or disciple. This blended model offers creative means of understanding and fulfilling the process of awakening.

The fundamental Yogacara Buddhist concepts are listed below using distinct descriptors for each: '0' for Twelve Links of the Chain of Causation, '1' for Nonduality, '2' for Dualistic pairs, '3' for the Three Aspects of Awakening, '4' for the Four Awakenings, and '8' for the eight components of Alayavijñāna storehouse consciousness. This method aids in memorizing them, and shows how the symbol captures their relationship and interaction.

'0' The reality of the Twelve Links of the Chain of Causation symbolized by the circle and names of the stages

- Conditioned states arise from within Alayavijñāna storehouse consciousness. They manifest as Ignorance, the 1st link of the Chain of Causation, and influence the 2nd link of Activity and Behavior
- A synonym for Ignorance (in the Buddhist sense) is Potentiality from within all forms of conditioning arises
- Though the causes of phenomena inevitably come to an end, the underlying conditions of the Twelve Links are more basic and have no discernible beginning or end

'1' The inclusive ellipse symbolizes Nonduality

- The totality of all physical and mental activities, good and bad, pleasant and distasteful, etc., are contained within the ellipse
- All Activity and Behavior contained within the ellipse can be viewed with Zazen-magnified awareness

'2' Dualistic pairs are symbolized by the ellipse that requires two focus points in order to draw it.

- All dualistic pairs such as delusion and enlighten-ment, and conditioned states and awakening, are complementary pairs
- The Personal and Universal Aspects of Mind are a complementary pair that together constitute an individual
- Nonduality is the complementary sum of dualistic pairs
- Daily life reflects the creative interplay of the complementary pair of conditioned states and their associated mental afflictions and awakening.

'3' Three Aspects of Awakening – the equilateral triangle depicts the three aspects of awakening

- The activity body of Nirmanakaya (Deconstruction): resolving conditioned states and gaining liberation – intuitive perception
- The reward body of Sambhogakaya (Reconstruction): integrating and refining gained freedom – cultivating and living the changes
- The reality body of Dharmakaya (Unencumbered Activity): living freedom – realization
- The three bodies are inseparable, of equal value, and engage in intimate and unending relations

'4' Four Awakenings – awakenings take place where the lines of Meditative Awareness intersect the sides of the triangle

Deconstruction

- Ability to observe the operation of a conditioned state '**a**'
- Resolution of a conditioned state results in freedom from the confinement of afflictive emotions associated with it, replaced by the liberation of thusness '**A**'

Reconstruction

- Ability to observe and begin the integration of the changes, and to fully embody the transformative change of being '**Aa**'
- Recognition that changes are completely integrated making responses to life natural and in accord with the needs of oneself and others. '**AA**'

'**8**' Alayavijñāna Storehouse Consciousness

Yogacara Buddhism teaches that within the storehouse consciousness an infinite number of possibilities exist in inactive storage, each one capable of becoming conscious. Conditioning associated with the personal and universal character of every being, when triggered brings about a change in conscious behavior and activity, with pleasant or adverse results. Some outcomes can be understood in a personal way, because they can be related to actions or experience of the existing person. The others that cannot be understood personally are rooted in the universal, and the mystery of time clouds their source. Understanding personal conditioned states allows a tie back to this-life experience; universal conditioning presents a daunting gap; effects are clear and obvious but with no discernible connection within the life experience of the living person.[18]

II. The Direct Perception of Zazen[19]

The practice of Zazen pictured as the "Meditative Landscape" consists of three components:

1、 The fundamental awareness of the Personal Aspect of Mind

2、 The response by the Universal Aspect of Mind aroused by the stimulus of willful awareness

3、 The complementary relationship of the Personal and Universal Aspects of Mind that manifests as intuitive perception, otherwise known as Prajna, Wisdom, or Thusness.

Shakyamuni Buddha taught in the Lankavatara Sutra that in Buddhist meditation the intuitive mind, also known as the faculty of intuition, arises from the purity of the Universal Aspect of Mind, and acts as the mediator between the Personal and Universal Aspects of Mind.

The essential activity of introspection of the Clean Language questions of Emergent Knowledge cultivates the relationship of the Personal and Universal Aspects of Mind. The five step-by-step statements below summarize how the relationship of the Personal and Universal Aspects matures from a practitioner's first acknowledgement of the Universal, and develops in time into a dialogue of unobstructed harmony.

1、 Recognizing the reality of the Universal Aspect of Mind – the experiential reality of conditioned states

2、 Establishing an intuitive engagement with the Universal Aspect of Mind — observation of the relationship of conditioned states and awakening

3、 Attaining an open relationship with the Universal Mind – resolution of a conditioned state

4、 The Personal and Universal Aspects of Mind intimately communicate refining the Personal Aspect of Mind – the inner dialogue becomes natural and beneficial

5、 The Personal and Universal Aspects of Mind act in unobstructed harmony – Unencumbered Activity

III. Inference and the Resolution Sequence[20]

The Resolution Sequence is an expedient to self-discovery, developed using Grove's Metaphor Therapy and the basic principles of Yogacara Buddhism. It provides a detailed description and step-by-step explanation of the process of awakening. The Resolution Sequence is made up of twelve stages that elaborate the three processes of awakening of Deconstruction, Reconstruction, and Unencumbered Activity, detailing and directing the operation of the four awakenings.

Each awakening consists of three elements of the Resolution Sequence – one that prepares the ground, the awakening itself, and the third that validates its occurrence. Following the sequence to completion results in the freedom of Unencumbered Activity and opens the pathway for resolving other life issues.

Deconstruction identifies and resolves conditioned states; Reconstruction focuses on integrating the freedom found in their resolution.

The Resolution Sequence and the embedded practices of reason, reflection, and fundamental awareness connect direct experience with the Sutra's definitive "Buddha's Word." Buddha's Word provides the conceptual understanding that clarifies the truth or falsity of direct experience. Inferences drawn from the Resolution Sequence act as a bridge between Direct Perception and the Sutras.

The three basic elements of Direct Perception in Zazen are contained in the geometric patterns of the Nonduality Symbol – Resolution Sequence Symbol.

Awakening 'a' Identification – Separation – Development
Awakening 'a' is a change of perspective produced within

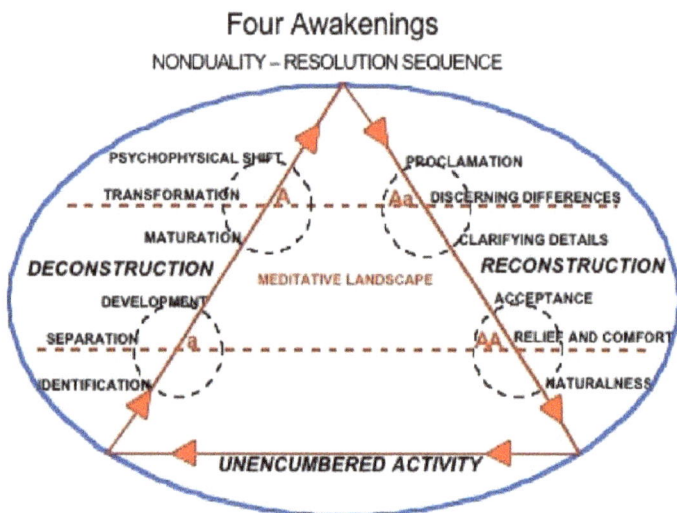

Four Awakenings
NONDUALITY – RESOLUTION SEQUENCE

PSYCHOPHYSICAL SHIFT

TRANSFORMATION

MATURATION

DECONSTRUCTION

DEVELOPMENT

SEPARATION

IDENTIFICATION

MEDITATIVE LANDSCAPE

PROCLAMATION

DISCERNING DIFFERENCES

CLARIFYING DETAILS

RECONSTRUCTION

ACCEPTANCE

RELIEF AND COMFORT

NATURALNESS

UNENCUMBERED ACTIVITY

Zazen practice that transforms one's worldview from "mundane only" to witnessing the sacred. Awakening 'a' is the gradual understanding of the reality of conditioned states and how they produce afflictive emotions. The effort to awaken is aroused only when awareness of the Universal Mind has strength and power: awareness of the truth of the Twelve Links of the Chain of Causation, and how its functions provide that power. In the stage of Identification, a growing awareness of one's existential predicament motivates the practice of Zazen that unveils the Universal Mind. Attaining Separation means accepting the Universal Mind as real. This is a life-changing event, simultaneously providing an observational space between oneself, conditioned states, and their reactive emotional responses.

Awakening 'A' Maturation – Transformation – Psychophysical Shift

In Maturation, the conditioned state is impartiality embraced, establishing the creative tension that is the motivating force of Transformation. Awakening 'A' launches practitioners into a new world where the stranglehold of the conditioned state is suddenly and permanently uprooted, unburdening them of the mental habits and deep-seated assumptions embedded in the conditioned state. Such breakthroughs generally are sudden events. Feelings of release, openness, and relaxation replace physical and mental constraints. The Universal Aspect of Mind comes compellingly to the forefront, precipitating a change of being.

Awakening 'Aa' Proclamation – Discerning Differences – Clarifying Details

The habit energies of an entrenched conditioned state do not completely dissolve at Transformation. Awakening 'Aa' is a new perspective that step-by-step discerns the differences between freedom and affliction. When the physical or mental remnants of the conditioned state appear, they are experienced as rootless and ephemeral. These habitual patterns associated with the conditioned states no longer cause afflictive responses. The vestigial habit energies draw attention but without influence or control. The Universal and Personal Minds beneficially interact, refining the attributes of the Personal.

Awakening 'AA' Acceptance – Relief and Comfort – Naturalness

Awakening 'AA' is a change of behavior. Habit energies dissipate. The Personal and Universal attain unity acting as complements with unobstructed harmony. It is the Middle Way of Buddhism, where the Personal (the mind of discrimination) and Universal (the mind of unity) manifest with equal importance.

Zazen Introspection – Resolution Sequence

The Resolution Sequence puts into words an introspective method that instructs practitioners in working with conditioned states. Introspective analysis into the operation and resolution of conditioned states naturalizes the inner dialogue between the Personal and Universal Aspects of Mind. Observation and questioning continue their definitive roles as the chief means of gathering experiential evidence. Acquiring conscious knowledge of conditioned states provides the basis for understanding the appropriate time and place for willful activities to avoid wasteful efforts. Understanding of the Nonduality – Resolution Sequence Chart is greatly enhanced by familiarity with:

- The complementary interplay of conditioned states and awakening[21]
- The Resolution Sequence developed in *Tending the Fire: An Introspective Guide to Zen Awakening*
- The symbols developed in *Becoming Literate in the Process of Awakening.*

Section 6
The Emergent Knowledge Summary Symbol

"Zen Masters have said that in complete perfect enlightenment
there are eighteen great awakenings
and countless minor awakenings.
A Zen proverb says, 'Those in a hurry do not arrive.'"

The Two Essentials for Working with Conditioned States

1、 Understands the complementary interplay between conditioned states and awakening (the Personal inquiry and Universal response)

2、 Experiences how the relationship of the Personal and Universal Aspects of Mind matures from a beginner's first acknowledgement of the Universal and develops into a dialogue of unobstructed harmony

Emergent Knowledge Sessions

I. Pre-Emergent Knowledge (1st Awakening) **'a'**
Identifies and observes the operation of a conditioned state and creates a Want Statement

II. Emergent Knowledge (2nd Awakening) **'A'**
Performs Emergent Knowledge "Clean" questioning

III. WDIKN (3rd Awakening) **'Aa'**
Creates "Proclamation" statement by answering, "What do I know now that I didn't know before?" and documents engagement with elements of Reconstruction. Compares "before and after" and notes the intensity and frequency of habit energies. Refinement of the dialogue between the Personal and Universal Aspects of Mind takes place

IV. Living Freedom (4th Awakening) **'AA'**
   Enjoys life and looks for new opportunities

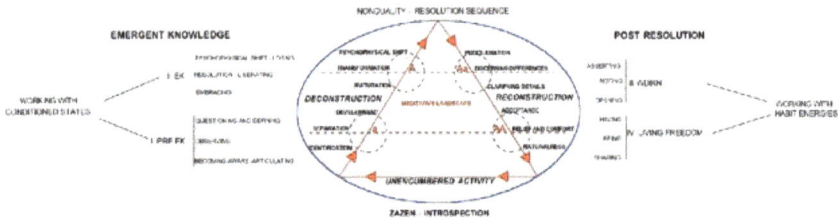

IMPORTANT POINTS IN EMERGENT KNOWLEDGE

I. Pre-Emergent Knowledge Questioning
Cultivate a deep and wide understanding of all aspects of the conditioned state that has your attention. Take a long time to thoroughly grasp the effects of the conditioned state on your life and only then formulate a Want Statement.

II. Within Emergent Knowledge Questioning
Approach Emergent Knowledge sessions with a calm deliberate mind. Cultivate awareness of the intimate spot where the information arises. Ask the questions as described and record the responses without analysis or reflection.

III. Working with Habit Energies
Answering the WDIKN question begins the growth and integration of the nascent freedom gained in the Emergent Knowledge session. Thoroughly involve yourself in comparing

the Want Statement goal with what actually exists. The effort at discernment and clarification should be given full attention in stillness sitting and moving meditation.

When conditioned states are stimulated, they present themselves as afflictive emotions or cognitive dissonance. After successful Emergent Knowledge sessions, habitual patterns of behavior and reaction persist but the negativity associated with them is greatly reduced or at times altogether dispelled. During Reconstruction, the habit energies leftover from the resolved conditioned state, manifest as distractions rather than reactive responses. Progress in Reconstruction is assessed by the decrease in strength and frequency of the appearance of habit energies connected with the resolved conditioned state. They weaken during Reconstruction through a consistent and steady awareness.

IV. Living Freedom – Realized when freedom becomes your own

One of the most difficult turnabouts for practitioners is to revere the "nonfabricated voice of nature" that is the relationship of the Personal and Universal Aspects of Mind. The nonfabricated voice speaks clearly, but doubt as to its veracity lies deep within habitual skepticism and unnoticed familiarity. Spiritual benefactor #28 of the Flower Ornament Sutra Ananyagamin counsels:

> *"This point is hard for celestial, human and titanic beings, for monks and priests ...... It cannot be heard or retained or believed in or comprehended by those who are not under the tutelage of spiritual benefactors, who have not accumulated roots of goodness, who have not purified their intentions, ... who do not have the eye of wisdom."*

The outer teacher of observing the critical phrase and/or the inner one of Emergent Knowledge provide the tutelage; the goodness and intention must be developed before starting on the journey; and the eye of wisdom opens with Zazen's capability to give rise to authentic vision.

Section 7
Documentation of Emergent Knowledge

All information connected with the Emergent Knowledge session should be documented using the Documentation of Emergent Knowledge Sheet (p. 24) or an equivalent. EK practitioners should carry a notebook so that thoughts and reflections that arise can be recorded and later transferred to the documentation sheet.

I. The required information includes:

1、 An identified, observed, and studied conditioned state

2、 A Want Statement (s) based on the conditioned state (or a WDIKN responses in multiple round sessions)

3、 Clean Language responses

4、 Answer(s) to a WDIKN question(s)

5、 All intuitions, reflections, and inferences that arise during Reconstruction

II. Recording Information

1、 Enter a description of the conditioned state to be used in the top row boxes.

2、 Formulate a Want Statement from the conditioned state and enter in Round 1 "Want Statement."

3、 Record each Clean Language response.

4、 Enter Round 1 answer to WDIKN. If this is the completion of the session, enter the WDIKN answer in Proclamation.

5、 For multiple round sessions, formulate a Want Statement using the previous Round's WDIKN. Then repeat items 3 and 4.

6、 For multiple Round sessions, the Proclamation is the last WDIK.

Documenting captures ephemeral insights and provides the framework for gauging progress, introspection, and in time, reveals hidden relationships. The thoroughness and accuracy of the documentation of the Reconstruction information determines the depth and speed of the assimilation of benefits from the session.

III. Major Points of Understanding for Reconstruction

1、 Proclamation: The WDIKN question is answered in the same manner as the Emergent Knowledge questions

2、 Discerning Differences focuses on the "before and after" of the Emergent Knowledge session to compare the Want Statement to present emotional and intellectual circumstances, and to notice the presence, frequency, and intensity level of habit energies.

3、 Clarifying Details: Continues work of Discerning Differences. Clarifying Details begins when the frequency and intensity of habit energies begins to decrease

4、 Acceptance: Acknowledges the enduring quality of the changes and weakening of habit energies

5、 Relief and Comfort: Practitioners note that habit energies associated with the conditioned state do not arise

6、 Naturalness: Lives freely without memory of conditioned state or habit energies

DOCUMENTATION EMERGENT KNOWLEDGE

What is the conditioned state?	How does the conditioned state affect me?	What is the conditioned state's trigger(s)?	Where in the body is the conditioned state located?		
Round 1 Want Statement	Round 2 Want Statement	Round 3 Want Statement	Round 4 Want Statement	Round 5 Want Statement	Round 6 Want Statement
1					
2					
3					
4					
5					
6					
WDIKN	WDIKN	WDIKN	WDIKN	WDIKN	WDIKN
Proclamation	Discerning Differences	Clarifying Details	Acceptance	Relief and Comfort	Naturalness

Metaphors in the
Buddhist Process of Awakening

EVERYDAY LIFE	CONCEPTUAL LIFE	INTIMACY OF THE PERSONAL AND UNIVERSAL ASPECTS OF MIND
Metaphors describe or compare two or more things or people.	Metaphors are rooted in concepts.	Metaphoric images and verbal articulations are concrete existence itself.
Metaphors enhance a description of an action or feeling.	The use of metaphors deepens conceptual understanding.	Metaphors are exact and precise expressions of the autonomous healing and awakening process.
Metaphors arise and take form in conversation and writing.	Metaphors describe relationships of conceptual elements.	Metaphors arise from the immediate relationship of inquiry and response.
Metaphors require a special talent to utilize.	Metaphors occur in every day encounters.	Metaphors are the language of awakening.
Metaphors are not necessary but add interest and nuance to expressions.	Metaphors proceed without difficulty from and within speech, reason, and thought.	Metaphors express the unity of the Personal and Universal Aspects of Mind.

The shaded area defines the metaphoric information that becomes apparent when working with the Proclamation Statement and beyond. The definitions of the unshaded columns are included to provide evidence on how the generation and use of metaphors evolves.

Endnotes

[1] This book references Thomas Cleary's translation of the Flower Ornament Sutra. See https://www.lionsroar.com/the-phenomenal-universe-of-the-flower-ornament-sutra/ for Taigen Dan Leighton's magazine article on Huayan Buddhism and the Phenomenal World of the Flower Ornament Sutra

[2] The benefactors are a democratic group consisting of goddesses, monks, lay householders, female, male, rich, and poor.

[3] See Enhanced Emergent Knowledge in this book for a basic understanding of the form and intent of inquiry and response.

[4] Gudo Nishijima, *Shobogenzo Book 3*, [BookSurge LLC, 2006 p.79]

[5] Renshin used *Visual Journaling: Going Deeper than Words*, by Susan Fox and Barbara Gamin, as her initial direction in learning to integrate verbal and visual intuition.

[6] Richard Wilhelm, Commentary on Hexagram #30, Li, The Clinging Fire, *I Ching* [New York, Bollingen Foundation, 1950 p. 119]

[7] There is some duplication of content because *Enhanced Emergent Knowledge* is based on the information contained within the *Emergent Knowledge and Zen Practice* booklet which proceeded it by a number of years.

[8] David Loy, *A New Buddhist Path*, [Somerville, MA: Wisdom Publications 2011, p. 137]

[9] See Robert Buswell's essay for detailed information on the history, development, and practice of observing the critical phrase. *The "Short-cut" Approach of Kan-hua Meditation: The Evolution of a Practical Subitism in Chinese Ch'an Buddhism,* contained within *Sudden and Gradual: Approaches to Enlightenment in Chinese Thought,* edited by Peter Gregory [Kuroda Institute 1987, pp. 322-378]

[10] Jeffrey Lyle Broughton, *The Letters of Zen Master Dahui Pujue* [New York, Oxford University Press, 2017, p. 133]

[11] Robert Buswell, *The "Short-cut" Approach of Kan-hua Meditation: The Evolution of a Practical Subitism in Chinese Ch'an Buddhism,* contained within *Sudden and Gradual: Approaches to Enlightenment in Chinese Thought*, edited by Peter Gregory [Kuroda Institute 1987, p. 348]

[12] Ibid, p. 349

[13] See Dale and Barbara Verkuilen, *Tending the Fire: An Introspective Guide to Zen Awakening* [Madison WI Firethroat Press 2011, pp. 1-18] for information on conditioned states

[14] Thomas Cleary, *The Blue Cliff Record* [Boston: Shambala, 2000, p. 72]

[15] See Dale Verkuilen, *Unfolding the Eightfold Path,* [Madison, WI Firethroat Press, 2014, pp. 27-33 for more information on the Informal Mind of sitting and the Formal Mind of movement.

[14] Jeffrey Lyle Broughton, *Zongmi on Chan*, [New York, Columbia University Press, 2009, p. 113]

[17] Dale and Barbara Verkuilen, *Tending the Fire: An Introspective Guide to Zen Awakening* [Madison WI Firethroat Press 2011, p. 40]

[18] '8' Yogacara Buddhism defines eight levels of consciousnesses: sight, sound, taste, touch, smell, consciousness, manas, and Alayavijñāna Storehouse Consciousness. The first seven arise from within and are functions of Alayavijñāna consciousness.

[19] The three basic elements of Direct Perception in Zazen are contained in the geometric patterns of the Nonduality Symbol – Resolution Sequence Symbol.

First, with the meditative landscape at its center, the symbol defines the practice of Zazen as fundamental awareness of all the activities of the self. Zazen provides a resourceful way of approaching the unity of inquiry and immediate insight. The faculty of intuition described by the Buddha operates as the mediator between the Personal and Universal Aspects of Mind. The mediating wisdom arises from within the Universal, and is brought to awareness by the mental discipline of Zazen. The enhanced vision of Zazen reveals the truth of the Universal Mind's existence, supplying the information and guidance to form a lucid and accurate depiction of the process of awakening. Engagement in Zazen sets the stage for the revolution of mind that cures the fundamental misperception of separateness.

Second, the triangle and arrowheads portray the dynamic movement of impermanence. Ongoing awareness of an endless stream of life cycles replaces the notion of the substantial and enduring self. Each fast-moving cycle contains both a unique problem based on the conditioning of the moment and the means to resolve it, and ultimately achieve liberation. Understanding and accepting the reality of the metabolism of this process transforms impermanence from a confining trap to an opportunity for ever- burgeoning freedom.

Third, the ellipse symbolizes the nondual complementary sum of the constant and vital interplay between the Personal and Universal aspects of life. The relationship of the body and mind in Zazen is an accessible example of the complementary interplay of the Personal and Universal Aspects. When sitting, an erect posture results in an aware mind, which in turn promotes an even straighter posture and so forth, in an endless positive feedback loop. Another is the "Clean Language" inquiry-response of Emergent Knowledge. The practitioner recognizes Nonduality to be the complementary activity of the body-mind or the inquiry and response, embracing all of the complexities and ambiguities of dualistic relationships.

[20] See Dale and Barbara Verkuilen, *Tending the Fire: An Introspective Guide to Zen Awakening* [Madison WI Firethroat Press 2011, pp. 41-42] for detailed information about the Resolution Sequence

[21] See Hee-Jin Kim, *Dogen and Meditation and Thinking* [Albany, NY State University of New York 2007 for Dōgen's teaching on the relationship of conditioned states [delusion] and awakening [enlightenment]

Author's Biography

Renshin Barbara Verkuilen trained as a psychotherapist, practicing for twenty years in various Wisconsin locations. She studied and practiced Zen Buddhism for fifty-five years under Rev. Soyu Matsuoka, Rev. Dainin Katagiri, and Rev. Shoken Winecoff, culminating in ordination as a Zen priest in 1997 and certification as a Zen teacher in 2013. She founded the Midwest Soto Zen Community in Madison in 2001, served at Ryumonji Zen Monastery, and at a number of Zen Centers in the Iowa, Minnesota, and Wisconsin on a temporary basis.

Renshin authored four books [The Tale of Zen Master Bho Li, Dokusan with Dōgen: Timeless Lessons in Negotiating the Way, Tending the Fire: An Introspective Guide to Zen Awakening, and Dancing with the Benefactors] and The Process of Awakening, a comprehensive study of Zen practice, as well as a number of guidebooks on Zen subject materials.

Her association with the psychotherapist, David Grove, and his non-interpretative, supposition-free approach to accessing intuitive knowledge, produced two innovative adaptations – Metaphor Awareness and Enhanced Emergent Knowledge –- both of which were integral to her counseling therapy and Zen practice.

Renshin's books are available at the usual sources and at www.Firethroatpress.com

www.ingramcontent.com/pod-product-compliance
Ingram Content Group UK Ltd.
Pitfield, Milton Keynes, MK11 3LW, UK
UKHW051522240125
4283UKWH00047B/772

9 798218 593575